Eliminating World Poverty:

Making Globalisation Work for the Poor

White Paper on International Development

D0709109

Presented to Parliament by the Secretary of State

for International Development

by Command of Her Majesty December 2000

Cm 5006

www.globalisation.gov.uk

Price £11.80

Eliminating World Poverty:

Making Globalisation Work for the Poor

White Paper on International Development

CONTENTS

Page

Foreword by the Prime Minister   6

Foreword by the Secretary of State
for International Development   7

Key Policy Commitments   10

CHAPTER 1

The Challenge of Globalisation
Reaffirming the International Development Targets   12
A second White Paper   13
The opportunities and risks of globalisation   14
Making globalisation work for the poor   19

CHAPTER 2

Promoting Effective Governments and Efficient Markets
Supporting effective government   23
Combating corruption   25
Effective government requires respect for human rights   26
Conflict prevents development and increases poverty   28
Making markets work for the poor   31

CHAPTER 3

Investing in People, Sharing Skills and Knowledge
Promoting better health for poor people   34
Spreading educational opportunity   36
Bridging the digital divide   39
Re-thinking the mobility of people   42
Encouraging pro-poor research   43
Intellectual property regimes and developing countries   44

CHAPTER 4

Harnessing Private Finance
The pattern of capital flows   48
Supporting sound domestic policies   49
Strengthening the international financial system   52
International co-operation on
   investment, competition and tax   55
Promoting corporate social responsibility   59
Encouraging private investment into
   developing countries   61

CHAPTER 5   *Capturing Gains from Trade*
                  Using trade to reduce poverty   65
                  Realising export potential   67
                  Creating a fairer international trading system
                     and reforming the WTO   69
                  Promoting a pro-development EU policy on trade   71
                  Helping poor people to trade   73
                  Making trade and non-trade standards
                     serve development   74

CHAPTER 6   *Tackling Global Environmental Problems*
                  Meeting our own responsibilities   77
                  Integrating environmental sustainability
                     into development planning   79
                  Working with the private sector   81
                  International co-operation on the environment   81

CHAPTER 7   *Using Development Assistance*
                  More Effectively
                  Focusing development assistance on
                     poverty reduction   84
                  Debt relief for poverty reduction   89
                  Nationally owned poverty reduction strategies   91
                  Improving the way development agencies
                     deliver assistance   92
                  Untying aid and promoting local procurement   94
                  Driving forward reform of European
                     Community assistance   95
                  Reforming the World Bank and the
                     Regional Development Banks   96
                  A more effective development role
                     for the United Nations   97

CHAPTER 8   *Strengthening the International System*
                  Reforming international institutions   99
                  A more effective voice for poor countries and people   100
                  Enlisting the G8, the OECD and the Commonwealth   100
                  Measuring progress   101
                  Strengthening the international response to conflict   102
                  Mobilising civil society   103
                  Making globalisation work for the poor   104

                  Source notes   106

                  Background Research Papers   108

FOREWORD BY THE PRIME MINISTER

One in five of the world's population - two thirds of them women - live in abject poverty, in a world of growing material plenty. The new millennium offers a real opportunity to eliminate world poverty. This is the greatest moral challenge facing our generation.

It is also in the UK's national interest. Many of the problems which affect us – war and conflict, international crime and the trade in illicit drugs, and the spread of health pandemics like HIV/AIDS – are caused or exacerbated by poverty.

Globalisation creates unprecedented new opportunities and risks. If the poorest countries can be drawn into the global economy and get increasing access to modern knowledge and technology, it could lead to a rapid reduction in global poverty – as well as bringing new trade and investment opportunities for all. But if this is not done, the poorest countries will become more marginalised, and suffering and division will grow. And we will all be affected by the consequences.

In order to make globalisation work for the poor we need not just strong and vibrant private sectors, but also effective governments and strong and reformed international institutions. We need to work collectively to tackle the problems of conflict and corruption, boost investment in education and health, spread the benefits of technology and research, strengthen the international financial system, reduce barriers to trade, tackle environmental problems and make development assistance more effective.

This White Paper sets out the UK Government's policies in all these areas. It reflects our commitment to work across all parts of Government in order to help eliminate world poverty, and to cooperate with other governments and international institutions as part of a broader international effort. It is consistent with our determination to tackle poverty and social exclusion in the UK.

We will work with vigour and determination and will take these issues to the highest level. The opportunity to eliminate poverty is within our reach. If we can grasp this, we can help build a world in which mass poverty will exist only as memory – and a world that is more stable and secure for our children and grandchildren.

Tony Blair

December 2000

FOREWORD BY THE SECRETARY OF STATE FOR INTERNATIONAL DEVELOPMENT

This second White Paper on International Development stands alongside our first - Eliminating World Poverty: A Challenge for the 21st Century. The first White Paper committed us to focus all our development effort on the reduction of poverty and the mobilisation of the international system to meet the International Development Targets.

We have spent the last three years working to achieve these objectives. We now have unprecedented consensus – across the UN system, the IMF and World Bank, most Regional Development Banks, leaders of developing countries, the G8 and the OECD – that the achievement of the Targets should be the focus of our joint endeavours. We have set out in our Target Strategy Papers how this can be done.

This Second White Paper analyses the nature of globalisation. It sets out an agenda for managing the process in a way that could ensure that the new wealth, technology and knowledge being generated brings sustainable benefits to the one in five of humanity who live in extreme poverty.

We are living at a time of profound historical change. Great wealth and great squalor exist side by side.

We could move forward to a period of massive progress and the removal of abject poverty from the human condition. Or we could see growing poverty, marginalisation, conflict and environmental degradation. Neither prospect is inevitable. The future is a matter of political will and change.

Cynicism and negativism are the enemies of progress. It is when people see that progress is possible that the demand for reform and advance is energised. I hope that this White Paper will help people of moral conscience and those with an intelligent concern for future generations - in all parts of the world - to join together to achieve a more decent and sustainable future for us all.

Clare Short
Secretary of State for International Development

December 2000

BOXES

CHAPTER 1

1. The International Development Targets   13

CHAPTER 2

2. Privatisation in Transition Economies   24
3. Combating Child Labour and Promoting Core Labour Standards   29

CHAPTER 3

4. The Impact of HIV/AIDS   35
5. The Prime Minister's Initiative   38
6. Commission on Intellectual Property Rights   46

CHAPTER 4

7. Transnational Corporations   50
8. Improving Global Financial Stability   55
9. Financial Instruments Supporting Investment in Developing Countries   62

CHAPTER 5

10. Globalisation, Jobs and Women   68

CHAPTER 6

11. Globalisation and Water Resources   80
12. Renewable Energy Initiative   82

CHAPTER 7

13. Improving the Allocation of Development Assistance   86
14. Global Public Goods   88
15. Simplifying and Harmonising Delivery of Development Assistance   93

CHAPTER 8

16. Development Policy Forums   104

FIGURES

CHAPTER 1

1.1 Progress towards the International Development Target: reducing the proportion of people living in extreme poverty by half between 1990 and 2015   21

1.2 Progress towards the other key International Development Targets   22

CHAPTER 3

3.1 The primary education challenge   37

3.2 Who uses the Internet?   39

CHAPTER 4

4.1 Net long term resource flows to developing countries   49

4.2 Bilateral Investment Treaties and Double Taxation Treaties concluded in 1999   57

CHAPTER 5

5.1 The relationship between trade and growth   66

5.2 Poverty is related to remoteness   73

CHAPTER 6

6.1 Energy efficiency tends to improve as income rises… …but overall consumption is much higher in richer countries   78

CHAPTER 7

7.1 Total flows per capita by region, 1998   85

7.2 Total flows per capita by income group, 1998   85

7.3 Global aid flows per poor person, 1998   86

KEY POLICY COMMITMENTS

THE CHALLENGE OF GLOBALISATION

The UK Government will:

- Work with others to manage globalisation so that poverty is systematically reduced and the International Development Targets achieved.
- Promote economic growth that is equitable and environmentally sustainable.

PROMOTING EFFECTIVE GOVERNMENTS AND EFFICIENT MARKETS

The UK Government will:

- Help developing countries build the effective government systems needed to reform their economic management, make markets work for poor people, and meet the challenge of globalisation.
- Work to reduce corruption, and ensure respect for human rights and a greater voice for poor people.
- Work with others to reduce violent conflict, including through tighter control over the arms trade.

INVESTING IN PEOPLE, SHARING SKILLS AND KNOWLEDGE

The UK Government will:

- Promote better health and education for poor people, and harness the new information and communications technologies to share skills and knowledge with developing countries.
- Help focus more of the UK and global research effort on the needs of the poor, and make intellectual property regimes work better for poor people.

HARNESSING PRIVATE FINANCE

The UK Government will:

- Work with developing countries to put in place policies that will attract private financial flows and minimise the risk of capital flight.
- Work to strengthen the global financial system to manage the risks associated with the scale, speed and volatility of global financial flows, including through use of 'road maps' to guide countries on opening of their capital accounts.
- Encourage international co-operation on investment, competition and tax that promotes the interests of developing countries.
- Encourage corporate social responsibility by national and transnational companies, and more investment by them in developing countries.

CAPTURING GAINS FROM TRADE

The UK Government will:

- Support an open and rules-based international trading system, and work to promote equitable trade rules and an effective voice for developing countries.
- Support continuing reductions in barriers to trade, both in developed and developing countries, and work to improve the capacity of developing countries to take advantage of new trade opportunities.

TACKLING GLOBAL ENVIRONMENTAL PROBLEMS

The UK Government will:

- Work to reduce the contribution made by developed countries to global environmental degradation.
- Work with developing countries to ensure that their poverty reduction strategies reflect the need to manage environmental resources sustainably, and strengthen their capacity to participate in international negotiations.

USING DEVELOPMENT ASSISTANCE MORE EFFECTIVELY

The UK Government will:

- Increase its development assistance to 0.33% as a proportion of GNP by 2003/04, and continue to make progress towards the 0.7% UN target.
- Work to increase the proportion of global development assistance spent in poor countries, help to improve its effectiveness and to reduce the burdens placed on recipient countries, end UK tied aid and work for multilateral untying.
- Introduce a new Development Bill to replace the outdated Overseas Development and Co-operation Act (1980), to consolidate our poverty focused approach to development.
- Provide faster and more substantial debt relief for heavily indebted poor countries that are committed to poverty reduction.

STRENGTHENING THE INTERNATIONAL SYSTEM

The UK Government will:

- Work with others to build a stronger, more open and accountable international system, in which poor people and countries have a more effective voice.

The Challenge of Globalisation

The UK Government will:

- **Work with others to manage globalisation so that poverty is systematically reduced and the International Development Targets achieved.**

- **Promote economic growth that is equitable and environmentally sustainable.**

Reaffirming the International Development Targets

1. One in five of the world's population – two-thirds of them women – live in abject poverty: on the margins of existence, without adequate food, clean water, sanitation or healthcare, and without education. That is 1.2 billion people whose lives are blighted by poverty, robbed of their dignity in a world of growing wealth and material plenty.

2. Three years ago the Government published its first White Paper on international development - *Eliminating World Poverty: a Challenge for the 21st Century*. After years in which development policy was subordinated to commercial and short-term political interests, the UK's development strategy is now focused on the reduction of abject poverty in the world.

3. At the heart of this agenda is a commitment to focus all of our development effort on the achievement of the International Development Targets — targets agreed by the governments of the world at a series of United Nations conferences in the 1990s (see box 1). As a first step towards the complete elimination of poverty, the targets include a reduction by one half in the proportion of people living in extreme poverty by 2015. As we move towards this, we will of course need to set further targets, in order to achieve the total elimination of extreme poverty.

4. In this Paper we strongly reaffirm the UK Government's commitment to the International Development Targets set out in our first White Paper. They remain absolutely central to our development strategy, including the policies we pursue through multilateral institutions. In three years we have made real progress in getting greater commitment to these targets across the international system.

5. The targets have been endorsed by the World Bank and the International Monetary Fund, by the European Union and by 77 African, Caribbean and Pacific countries as part of the Cotonou agreement and by the Development Assistance Committee of the Organisation for Economic Co-operation and Development (OECD). Most recently, many of the targets were also endorsed by 149 Heads of State at the UN Millennium Summit in New York.

BOX 1

THE INTERNATIONAL DEVELOPMENT TARGETS

The International Development Targets are:

- A reduction by one half in the proportion of people living in extreme poverty by 2015.
- Universal primary education in all countries by 2015.
- Demonstrated progress towards gender equality and the empowerment of women by eliminating gender disparity in primary and secondary education by 2005.
- A reduction by two-thirds in the mortality rates for infants and children under age 5 and a reduction by three-fourths in maternal mortality – all by 2015.
- Access through the primary healthcare system to reproductive health services for all individuals of appropriate ages as soon as possible, and no later than the year 2015.
- The implementation of national strategies for sustainable development in all countries by 2005, so as to ensure that current trends in the loss of environmental resources are effectively reversed at both global and national levels by 2015.

There is now an unprecedented international consensus around these targets.

6. The targets are challenging, some particularly so. But if we put in place the right policies, nationally and internationally, we believe that they are achievable. It should be noted, however, that they can be achieved overall but missed in some countries. Progress is dependent on national governments in all countries strengthening their commitment to poverty reduction.

7. In the last few decades, there has been enormous progress in development. Since the 1960s, life expectancy in developing countries has risen from 46 to 64 years, infant mortality rates have halved, there has been an increase of more than 80 per cent in the proportion of children enrolled in primary school, and there has

been a doubling of access to safe drinking water and basic sanitation[i].

8. Over this period, we have learned a lot about what works in development – and about what does not. Our task is to apply these lessons on a larger scale in the context of globalisation. It is clear that development strategies must be adapted to local circumstances and must be nationally owned and nationally led by developing and transition countries[1]. But we believe that globalisation creates unprecedented new opportunities for sustainable development and poverty reduction, and for progress against the targets.

A second White Paper

9. This White Paper stands alongside our first White Paper, and our Target Strategy Papers which set out how each of the International Development Targets can be met. Its purpose is to focus on the

---

[1] *In the rest of this Paper, where the term 'developing countries' is used, the analysis also applies to transition countries.*

challenges of globalisation and to define a policy agenda for managing the process in a way that will systematically reduce poverty.

10. Encouragingly, in recent years we have seen the beginnings of a serious political debate about the equitable management of globalisation. Last year's Human Development Report and this year's reports by the UN Secretary General and by the World Bank have this as a core theme[ii].

11. As the Secretary General put it in his report to the Millennium Assembly, *'The central challenge we face today is to ensure that globalisation becomes a positive force for all the world's people, instead of leaving billions of them behind in squalor. Inclusive globalisation must be built on the great enabling force of the market, but market forces alone will not achieve it. It requires a broader effort to create a shared future, based upon our common humanity in all its diversity'*[iii].

12. Making globalisation work more effectively for the world's poor is a moral imperative. It is also in our common interest. Many of the world's contemporary challenges — war and conflict; refugee movements; the violation of human rights; international crime, terrorism and the illicit drugs trade; the spread of health pandemics like HIV/AIDS; and environmental degradation – are caused or exacerbated by poverty and inequality.

13. This mutual dependence is particularly clear in the case of population growth and environmental degradation. In the next 25 years around 2 billion people will be added to the world's population – 97 per cent of them in developing countries. There will be a further shift of population from the rural areas to the towns, with an estimated 61 per cent of the world's population living in urban areas by 2025[iv].

14. These demographic changes will create huge new demands. Managed badly, this could lead to growing conflicts over scarce resources, particularly water, and new social tensions that could easily spill over national borders. There can be no secure future for any of us – wherever we live – unless we promote greater global social justice.

15. Progress is dependent on developing country leadership. But some of the resources needed will have to be provided by the international community. A sustainable global environment and effective vaccines against communicable diseases are just two examples of the global public goods that can and should be financed internationally.

The opportunities and risks of globalisation

16. The word globalisation is used in different ways. The contested nature of the

THE CHALLENGE OF GLOBALISATION

concept is part of the explanation for the confusion of so much of the public debate. For some, globalisation is inextricably linked with the neo-liberal economic policies of the 1980s and early 1990s. For them, globalisation is synonymous with unleashing market forces, minimising the role of the state and letting inequality rip. They denounce the increasingly open and integrated global economy as an additional more potent source of global exploitation, poverty and inequality.

17. In fact, globalisation means the growing interdependence and inter-connectedness of the modern world. This trend has been accelerated since the end of the Cold War. The increased ease of movement of goods, services, capital, people and information across national borders is rapidly creating a single global economy. The process is driven by technological advance and reductions in the costs of international transactions, which spread technology and ideas, raise the share of trade in world production, and increase the mobility of capital. It is also reflected in the diffusion of global norms and values, the spread of democracy and the proliferation of global agreements and treaties, including international environmental and human rights agreements.

18. Globalisation is characterised, too, by the growth of transnational companies, which now account for about a third of world output and two-thirds of world trade. Around a third of world trade takes place within transnationals, between subsidiaries of the same corporation based in different countries.

19. Managed wisely, the new wealth being created by globalisation creates the opportunity to lift millions of the world's poorest people out of their poverty. Managed badly and it could lead to their further marginalisation and impoverishment. Neither outcome is predetermined; it depends on the policy choices adopted by governments, international institutions, the private sector and civil society.

20. Globalisation brings with it rapid change. And this has generated uncertainty and anxiety amongst millions of people across the world. It has also raised legitimate public concerns, for example about the impact of globalisation on people's culture, the environment, inequality within and between countries, and the effect on the world's poorest people. If democrats and internationalists do not address these concerns, then those who advocate narrow nationalism, xenophobia, protectionism and the dismantling of multilateral institutions will gain in strength and influence with disastrous consequences for us all.

21. To many people, the most visible impact of globalisation is the near universal availability of the same consumer goods –

such as soft drinks, hamburgers, popular music and television programmes. Some fear that this is leading to a single homogeneous culture dominated by western commodities and values.

22. However, throughout human history, exposure to outside influence has tended to enrich, rather than impoverish, individuals and societies. Globalisation has accelerated this process and produced elements of a 'global culture'. But it has also encouraged a re-assertion of local cultural identity and, in many cases, greater respect for diversity and pluralism.

23. English is emerging as a means of communicating internationally, but this does not pose a threat to the languages that are spoken in daily life in communities across the world. The risk of a global monoculture of values and aspirations is vastly greater if the developing world remains poor and marginalised rather than an equal and respected part of a rich international diversity of culture and language.

24. There is also concern that globalisation is damaging the global environment. It is certainly true that the global environment continues to deteriorate, and that many renewable resources – freshwater, forests, plant and animal species – are being exhausted at a rate beyond their natural recovery level. Seventy per cent of the world's fishing areas, for example, are over or fully fished, yet a billion people depend on fish as their main source of protein. It is also true that the consumption patterns of people in developed countries are the major source of global environmental degradation.

25. But this process was at work before global integration speeded up. Indeed openness and integration into the global economy can help countries to meet the new environmental challenges. Poverty and environmental degradation are often linked. Economic development gives countries improved access to new, less resource-intensive and less polluting technologies. Over the last fifty years, it has been more closed economies – such as the former Communist countries – that have had the worst record of industrial pollution and urban environmental degradation.

26. Stronger international institutions and a much stronger commitment to sustainable development at the national and the international level are needed to help the world shift to more sustainable patterns of production and consumption. But if the world remains deeply divided and the poorest countries believe that improved environmental standards will prevent or hinder their development, international agreement to protect global environmental resources will become impossible. A world commitment to sustainable development is dependent on the guarantee of development for the poor.

27. Many believe that globalisation causes rising levels of inequality and poverty. The best evidence to date suggests that there is no systematic relationship between openness and inequality, or between growth and inequality[v].

28. Take the question of inequality between countries. After increasing between 1960 and 1990, this has more recently started to fall. In 1960, the average real income in the countries containing the richest fifth of the world's population was 12 times greater than in the countries containing the poorest fifth; in 1990 it was 18 times greater; by the late 1990s this had fallen to 15 times greater[2].

29. The explanation for these figures lies in differences in economic performance. The world's richest countries have continued to grow; the world's two biggest nations – India and China, containing huge numbers of the world's poor – have accelerated their growth rates over the last two decades; while many of the poorest countries in Africa have stood still, or experienced negative growth. Whether inequality between countries rises or falls in the years ahead depends on the policies that they pursue. If the poorest countries improve their economic performance then global inequality should fall; if they do not, it is likely to rise.

30. Similarly within countries, the evidence indicates that there is no systematic relationship between increased openness and changes in inequality – in some cases the poor gain more from trade than the average citizen; in other cases they gain less.

31. Everywhere it is clear that openness is a necessary – though not sufficient – condition for national prosperity. No developed country is closed. The initially poor countries that have been most successful in catching up in recent decades – the newly industrialising east Asian countries and China – seized the opportunity offered by more open world markets to build strong export sectors and to attract inward investment. This contributed, along with massive investment in education, to the largest reduction in abject poverty that the world has ever seen. In most east Asian countries the proportion of the population living in poverty is now under 15 per cent, down from around 40 per cent forty years ago.

32. There is no systematic relationship between economic growth and inequality. Over recent decades, inequality has risen in some cases and fallen in others, in both fast-growing and slower-growing economies.

33. Through expanding access to ideas, technology, goods, services and capital, globalisation can certainly create the conditions for faster economic growth. And the progress which has been made

[2] The figures for 1960 and 1990 are drawn from the 1996 UNCTAD Report on Least Developed Countries. The figures for the late 1990s have been estimated by DFID using World Bank Indicators 2000 data, and are adjusted to form a consistent time series. All these figures are based on purchasing power parity comparisons. Purchasing power parity (ppp) is essentially a hypothetical exchange rate which equalises the buying power of currencies. With a dollar converted to another country's currency at the ppp exchange rate, you should on average be able to buy the same set of goods in that country as you could for one dollar in the USA.

over the last few decades in reducing the proportion of people living in poverty has been largely the result of economic growth: raising incomes generally, including those of poor people. Economic growth is an indispensable requirement for poverty reduction.

34. But by itself it is not enough. Pro-poor development requires growth *and* equity. Poverty reduction is faster where growth is combined with declining inequality. And poverty reduction is also more easily achieved in less unequal countries – the lower the level of inequality, the larger the share of the benefits of growth that accrue to the poor.

35. In practice the impact of globalisation on poor people varies widely, both between countries and within them, depending on initial circumstances and on the policies that governments pursue. Within China, for example, poor people living in coastal provinces have benefited more from increased exports and foreign investment than those in inland provinces. In Ghana, the lowering of barriers to trade let in imports of low-priced garments, many of them from China, which benefited poor consumers but displaced workers from garment factories.

36. The reality is that all profound economic and social change produces winners and losers. The role of government in these circumstances is to help manage the process of change – to maximise economic opportunities for all, and to equip people, through education and active labour market policies, to take advantage of these opportunities.

37. We must not forget that many of the world's poor people, living in remote or inaccessible rural areas of Africa and south Asia, have so far not been much affected by globalisation one way or the other. For them, the real risk is that they will be marginalised from the new wealth that globalisation is creating. That is why it is so important to design economic strategies that recognise and respect countries' specific needs and circumstances, and to promote sustainable and inclusive economic and social development that spreads its benefits to all sections of society.

38. Globalisation also brings some systemic risks. For example, the damaging effects of financial volatility were vividly illustrated in the Asian crisis of 1997. Greater access to the global pool of savings through capital markets offers developing countries the chance to raise growth rates above the levels that can be supported from domestic savings alone. But the Asian experience indicates clearly that openness to short-term portfolio flows can be damaging in the absence of a sound macroeconomic position, adequate domestic regulation and transparency in relationships between companies and banks. Strong and effective regulatory systems are needed at the national and the international level.

Making globalisation work for the poor

39. The UK Government believes that, if well managed, the benefits of globalisation for poor countries and people can substantially outweigh the costs, especially in the longer term. The rapid integration of the global economy, combined with advances in technology and science, is creating unprecedented global prosperity. And this has helped to lift millions of people out of poverty. With the right policies, many millions more people can benefit in the years ahead.

40. The following chapters set out our analysis of the issues and some of the suggested policy responses to them. Two overarching themes run throughout the remainder of this document.

41. First, the importance of political will. It is not inevitable that globalisation will work well for the poor – nor that it will work against them. This depends on the policies that governments and international institutions pursue. We need developing countries, developed countries, international institutions, the private sector and civil society to rise to the challenges of globalisation, to exploit better its opportunities and minimise its risks. Developing countries must lead the effort

for greater poverty reduction in their countries. But developed countries and international institutions must support them in this process.

42. Second, globalisation is reinforcing the need for a more integrated approach to policy-making. Policies no longer fit into neat sectoral boxes, and the distinction between domestic and international policy is increasingly blurred. Most 'domestic' policies such as taxation have international aspects, and most 'international' policies such as trade have domestic dimensions. The formulation of sustainable development strategies in a global economy requires that developed and developing countries have more joined-up and coherent policies.

43. There is a particular responsibility on developed countries. There is no sense, for example, in using development assistance to support countries, and then undermining this through trade restrictions and unfair subsidies. All developed country policies towards the world's poorest countries should be consistent with a commitment to sustainable development and poverty reduction.

44. If developing countries are to maximise the benefits of globalisation, they need effective systems of government and action against corruption; they need to ensure respect for human rights, and to promote security, safety and justice for all.

They need to prevent violent conflict. And they need to make markets work better for poor people. These issues are the focus of *Chapter 2*.

45. To succeed in the new global economy, poor countries need healthy and well-educated people, and greater access to knowledge, ideas and new information and communication technologies. And to reduce poverty more quickly, there needs to be a shift in the global research effort. This is the focus of *Chapter 3*.

46. Private financial flows can help poor countries boost their levels of economic growth and reduce poverty. But large-scale and volatile flows can also produce financial instability that can be damaging to development. Strategies to attract greater flows to poor countries, to promote global financial stability and to encourage corporate social responsibility are the focus of *Chapter 4*.

47. Open trade has a vital role to play in helping countries to reduce poverty. But to maximise these benefits, poor countries need a rules-based international trading system, with continuing reductions in barriers to trade in both developed and developing countries. These issues are the focus of *Chapter 5*.

48. Sustainable use of the environment is essential for poverty reduction. But the global environment continues to deteriorate, putting at risk the resources on which poor people depend for their livelihoods. We need to manage globalisation in a way that is consistent with environmental sustainability. This is the focus of *Chapter 6*.

49. Development assistance is essential to enable countries to create the economic and social conditions necessary for poverty reduction. This is particularly important for the poorest countries which do not attract large-scale private flows. But aid resources need to be better used. Debt relief also needs to be linked to strategies for poverty reduction. These issues are the focus of *Chapter 7*.

50. Where there are no rules, the rich and powerful bully the poor and the powerless. In a globalising world, poor countries need effective, open and accountable global institutions where they can pursue their interests on more equal terms. This is the focus of *Chapter 8*.

FIGURE 1.1

Progress towards the International Development Target: reducing the proportion of people living in extreme poverty by half between 1990 and 2015

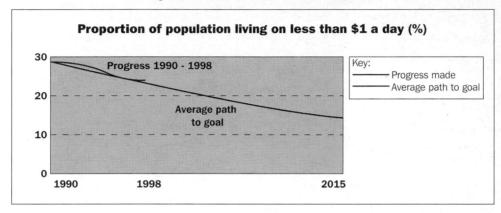

Proportion of population living on less than $1 a day (%)

Changes in population living on less than US$1 a day

Regions	Number of people living on less than $1 a day (millions)		Proportion of people living on less than $1 a day (percent)	
	1990	1998 (est.)	1990	1998 (est.)
East Asia and the Pacific	452	278	28	15
Eastern Europe and Central Asia	7	24	2	5
Latin America and the Caribbean	74	78	17	16
Middle East and North Africa	6	6	2	2
South Asia	495	522	44	40
Sub-Saharan Africa	242	291	48	46
Total Developing Countries	**1,276**	**1,199**	**29**	**24**

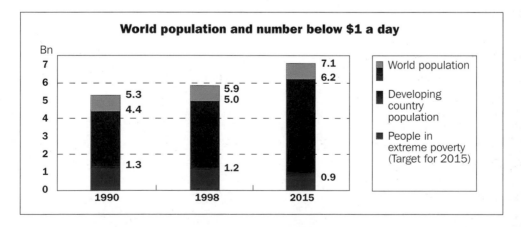

World population and number below $1 a day

Note: All data are at 1993 purchasing power parities. See footnote 2.
Source: 'A Better World for All' 2000 and World Bank, World Development Indicators 2000

FIGURE 1.2

Progress towards the other key International Development Targets

Enrol all children in primary school by 2015

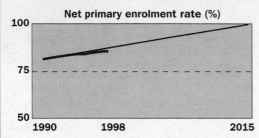

Net primary enrolment rate (%)

Although enrolment rates continue to rise, they have not risen fast enough. On current trends, more than 100 million school-age children will not be in school in 2015. Most of these children will be in Sub-Saharan Africa and South Asia. Other regions are much closer to the target - East Asia and the Pacific have almost achieved universal primary education.

Eliminate gender disparities in primary and secondary education by 2005

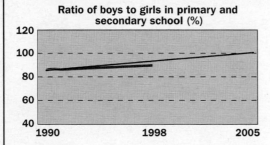

Ratio of boys to girls in primary and secondary school (%)

The gender gap is narrowing, but girls' enrolments remain persistently behind those of boys. Gender disparity is greatest in South Asia, closely followed by the Middle East and North Africa. In comparison, Latin America and the Caribbean has the greatest gender equality in both primary and secondary enrolment and in adult literacy.

Reduce infant and child mortality rates by two-thirds between 1990 and 2015

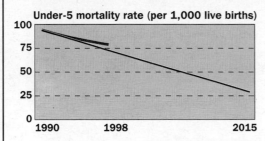

Under-5 mortality rate (per 1,000 live births)

Infant and under-5 mortality rates have fallen in all regions. But the fall is not enough to meet the target. Even in the best performing regions such as the Middle East and North Africa and Latin America and the Caribbean, there were major variations among countries. Overall, for every country that reduced infant and under-5 child mortality rates fast enough to reach the goal, ten lagged behind and another one moved backwards, often because of HIV/AIDS.

Reduce maternal mortality rates by three-quarters between 1990 and 2015

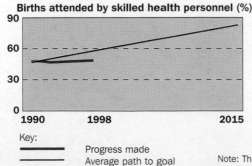

Births attended by skilled health personnel (%)

Provision of skilled care during pregnancy and delivery can do much to avoid many of the half million maternal deaths that occur each year, but the proportion of births attended by skilled personnel rose slowly in the 1990s. Maternal mortality varies widely among the world's regions - for instance, low in Latin America, but very high in Africa.

Key:

——————— Progress made
————— Average path to goal

Source: 'A Better World for All' 2000

Note: There are also International Development Targets on Reproductive Healthcare and on Sustainable Development and Environmental Resources.

CHAPTER 2

PROMOTING EFFECTIVE GOVERNMENTS AND EFFICIENT MARKETS

The UK Government will:

- **Help developing countries build the effective government systems needed to reform their economic management, make markets work better for poor people and meet the challenges of globalisation.**

- **Work to reduce corruption, and ensure respect for human rights and a greater voice for poor people.**

- **Work with others to reduce violent conflict, including through tighter control over the arms trade.**

Supporting effective government

51. Effective governments and efficient markets are both essential if developing countries are to reap the benefits of globalisation and to make that process work for poor people. While the market fundamentalism of the 1980s and early 1990s has been thoroughly discredited, it is now almost universally accepted that efficient markets are indispensable for effective development. But equally important are effective governments – which are both competent in carrying out their basic functions, and more accountable, responsive and democratic, with a bigger voice for poor people in the determination of government policy.

52. Globalisation gives added urgency to the task of strengthening government systems in developing countries. Private capital is highly mobile and will go to where business can be carried out safely and where it can make the best return. Weak and ineffective states, with problems of corruption, inadequate infrastructure and

cumbersome bureaucratic procedures, are not an attractive destination for these flows.

53. By contrast, those countries that apply rules and policies predictably, ensure law and order, invest in human capital (particularly education and health) and protect property rights, are likely to attract higher levels of inward investment and trade and to generate faster economic growth.

54. A key function of governments is the provision of law and order. And this is also a priority for the poor. One of the findings of the World Bank's *Voices of the Poor* report was that poor people attach enormous importance to security – security from violence and security for their property[vi]. Without this, they find it impossible to improve their lives. The poor worldwide also tend to be very distrustful of existing police and criminal justice systems. Far from protecting people from violence, too often elements within the police and justice systems are themselves sources of violence and abuse.

23

BOX 2

PRIVATISATION IN TRANSITION ECONOMIES

At the onset of transition ten years ago, there was some consensus that the existing state dominated economic model was unsustainable. However, there was much less understanding about how market economies function effectively, and about the complementary social and political institutions that are needed to help them do this.

Some central and eastern European countries, Hungary and Poland in particular, followed a strategy of creating favourable conditions for bottom-up development of the private sector. Strengthening institutions and creating sound legal and regulatory frameworks to ensure security of private ownership and eliminate barriers to entry were the priorities. In addition, the consistent enforcement of bankruptcy and accounting laws led to profitable companies being bought by investors and loss making ones being forced into liquidation. The negative effect of rising unemployment on poverty levels was mitigated to some extent by social safety net provisions.

By contrast, in countries of the former Soviet Union there was no experience of alternative economic systems. In Russia, for instance, the transition to private ownership was based on the rapid elimination of some elements of state ownership. State assets were dispersed through voucher schemes only to end up concentrated in large investment funds owned by state-owned banks or with privileged businessmen. Private interest groups exercised huge influence on the government and opposed legal and regulatory reform. This process generated opportunities for corruption. Special privileges and exemptions granted to Russian oligarchs have distorted market-orientated institutions and crowded out new enterprises. Simultaneously, production levels have plummeted. Corporate government remains weak and enterprise restructuring has barely begun. With enterprises no longer providing a social safety net, a massive increase in hidden unemployment and poverty had accompanied the economic collapse.

This experience demonstrates conclusively that economic reform must be accompanied by the right political institutions and a transparent legal framework. Only then can new enterprises create sufficient employment to offset the loss of jobs resulting from public sector restructuring. More foreign direct investment will flow in, stimulate competition and contribute to economic growth. Supportive social policies have to be in place to ease the impact of transition and to train and equip the labour force for new employment opportunities.

55. Safety and security depend on the fair and effective enforcement of the rule of law – to protect the rights of individuals against each other and against the state, and to uphold contracts. The absence of an effective rule of law is a barrier to the proper functioning of a market economy, a deterrent to domestic and foreign investment, and a breeding ground for corruption. For example, many banks in developing countries will not provide loans for tractors, sewing machines or other investments in small enterprise, if there is no legal system to enforce the agreements made.

56. Effective governments are needed to build the legal, institutional and regulatory framework without which market reforms can go badly wrong, at great cost – particularly to the poor. Whilst excessive or cumbersome regulatory barriers stifle incentives and discourage investment, effective regulation remains essential – for instance to promote financial sector stability, to protect consumers, to safeguard the environment, and to promote and protect human rights, including core labour standards.

57. Effective governments are also needed to put in place good social policies. Only the state can ensure the provision of key public services. Of course, the state does not need to be involved in the direct provision of all public services. The commercial and voluntary sectors have an important contribution to make to service delivery. But the unique and indispensable role of government remains that of setting policies and priorities, ensuring that basic services are provided to all, and regulating to ensure quality and standards.

58. The way in which governments allocate public revenues – between different public services and between services and other spending priorities – has a major impact on the level of poverty reduction. It is vital that poor people should have a greater say over governments' spending decisions.

59. The UK Government, through its development effort and contributions to international development agencies, is working to help countries put in place political and legal reforms, reforms to the civil service and systems of public administration, and tax collection. We also support reforms to police and criminal justice systems, that make them more accessible and responsive to the needs of the poor.

Combating corruption

60. More effective government and greater benefits from markets require tougher action – by developing and developed countries – to deal with corruption. The evidence suggests that investment levels are lower in countries with high levels of corruption, due to the uncertainty created, the cost of bribes and time-consuming bureaucracy[vii].

61. It is poor people who suffer most from corruption. Essential medicines are diverted; unofficial payments are commonly required for water and electricity connections, as well as education and healthcare; and the police and the judiciary often respond only to bribery.

62. Often this 'petty corruption' is accompanied by 'grand corruption', involving leaders, politicians, senior officials and entrepreneurs. This can take many forms. Bribes may flow from international firms in order to win contracts or seek other favours from politicians and officials. This is often particularly acute in areas involving the allocation of natural resource concessions and their revenues. Sometimes the corruption involves looting public assets within the country. This process leads to distorted decision-making, discriminatory application of regulations, tax evasion and resources wasted on poor projects – all of which damage the prospects for development and poverty reduction and the ability of poor countries to compete in a global economy.

63. Individuals involved in large-scale corruption must be caught and prosecuted but such individuals exist in all societies. What developing countries lack are effective systems of financial management, procurement and accountability.

64. The UK Government is committed to supporting developing countries in their efforts to implement effective anti-corruption strategies. To put our own house in order, we will legislate to give UK courts jurisdiction over UK nationals who commit offences of corruption abroad. The new legislation will put beyond doubt the consistency of UK law with the OECD Convention on the Bribery of Foreign Public Officials, and make it clear that bribes – wherever they are paid – are not tax deductible.

65. Grand corruption is also closely supported by global money laundering, Corruptly acquired money is recycled through the global financial system so that it reappears 'laundered' as apparently legitimately held funds in respectable banks in the developed world.

66. We will introduce legislation to strengthen the law on money laundering, ensure financial institutions uphold their commitments under the legislation and establish good practice, and permit the restraint of assets at an earlier stage in the investigative process[viii]. We are jointly funding with the European Commission an initiative under the auspices of the Asia/Europe Meeting (ASEM) to develop anti-money laundering strategies in ten Asian countries. We have also provided support for anti-money laundering collaboration between Caribbean countries and in eastern and southern Africa.

67. We are also committed to greater co-operation with developing and transition countries to help them recover funds that were illegally acquired through criminal activity or corruption and subsequently deposited in the UK. We plan to strengthen the arrangements which give overseas governments access to the courts and investigative authorities in the UK so that they can pursue claims to evidence and assets more effectively. Through our development assistance programmes, we will provide advice to governments on preparing their requests. And we are working with other countries to develop an appropriate policy framework for leading financial centres to assist with the recovery of stolen assets.

Effective government requires respect for human rights

68. Globalisation has been associated with a growth in democracy. The

PROMOTING EFFECTIVE GOVERNMENTS AND EFFICIENT MARKETS

proportion of countries with forms of democratic government has risen from 28 per cent in 1974 to 61 per cent in 1998[ix]. Moreover improved global communication has facilitated greater international solidarity in support of democratic freedoms and human rights. Information is circulated more widely within civil society. People everywhere are better informed about developments elsewhere. Abuses are given global publicity. And, increasingly, governments have to explain their actions and omissions to a global audience.

69. This spread of democratic structures represents a crucial advance. But the existence of the formal structures of democracy – political parties, elections, and parliaments – does not guarantee the empowerment of poor people, even when they make up a majority of the population. A poor majority often lacks influence because power is held by a narrow elite, with rulers exercising power through support from a regional group, through social status or through concentrated wealth.

70. Making political institutions work for poor people means helping to strengthen the voices of the poor and helping them to realise their human rights. It means empowering them to take their own decisions, rather than being the passive objects of choices made on their behalf. And it means removing forms of discrimination – in legislation and government policies – that prevent poor people from having control over their own

lives and over the policies of governments. Governments must be willing to let people speak, and to develop mechanisms to ensure that they are heard. This is central to what we mean by a rights based approach to development.

71. The voices of the poor can be strengthened by supporting those parts of civil society that help poor people organise to influence decision makers. The new information and communications technologies also have a role in strengthening the voices of poor people. A free press and broadcast media, capable of challenging government policies and their impact on the poor, is crucial. The interests of the poor also require inclusive and fair electoral processes and controls on election spending. And they require parliaments that scrutinise legislation and control the budgeting process, and hold to account the policy of the executive.

72. Development requires the empowerment of women. Huge progress was made in the 20th century, with women enjoying greater freedom and power than ever before. But they still lag behind men in virtually all aspects of life. Up to seventy per cent of the world's poor are women. Gender discrimination is the most widespread form of social exclusion and discrimination. Inequalities are to be found in economic and human development, and in political representation. There can be no equitable globalisation without greater equality and empowerment for women.

73. Action is required to address the needs of children and to implement the UN Convention on the Rights of the Child. Globalisation has the potential to enhance the welfare of children, but too many children in today's world continue to live in abject poverty. Too many children have their most basic human rights violated on a daily basis – whether through lack of adequate nutrition, limited access to education and healthcare, or through exposure to violence and abuse.

74. A large number of children also suffer from what we might call the 'dark side' of globalisation – the growing pornography industry and the trade in child prostitutes. This has been facilitated by modern communications technology, including the Internet. In some parts of the world, children are press-ganged to serve in armies as child soldiers. And there are millions of child labourers, some of them working in extremely hazardous and dangerous conditions (see box 3).

75. Children born today will be fifteen years of age in 2015. To achieve the 2015 targets it is essential to break the cycle of poverty and disadvantage – providing opportunities for today's children that were denied to their parents. We need to ensure that children are educated so that they can take advantage of opportunities, and receive the protection they need from disease and abuse to allow them to build their own and their country's future.

76. The UK Government is committed to working with others to enhance the human rights of poor people. Through our development programmes and our diplomatic efforts we will continue to encourage governments around the world to ratify the UN human rights treaties, to help them abide by the obligations that those treaties place on states, and to put them into practice in national legislation and policy.

Conflict prevents development and increases poverty

77. Promoting effective and inclusive systems of government, including an accountable security sector, is an essential investment in the prevention of violent conflict. The promotion of peace and stability is indispensable if countries are to attract investment and trade, and promote pro-poor development.

78. Violent conflict is one of the biggest barriers to development in many of the world's poorest countries. Of the 40 poorest countries in the world, 24 are either in the midst of armed conflict or have only recently emerged from it. This problem is particularly acute in Africa where twenty per cent of the population live in countries affected by armed conflict. Armed conflict also leads to population displacement. It is estimated that 10.6 million people in Africa are internally displaced – the majority of them uprooted by war.

PROMOTING EFFECTIVE GOVERNMENTS AND EFFICIENT MARKETS

BOX 3

COMBATING CHILD LABOUR AND PROMOTING CORE LABOUR STANDARDS

One of the most widespread public concerns about globalisation is its impact on labour standards. Across the world, millions of people – children and adults – work in conditions which are hazardous and abusive. They may be subject to sexual harassment, exploitative hours or wages, physical dangers and, in the worst cases, imprisonment and violence. Globalisation is both raising poor people's awareness of their rights in the workplace, and alerting consumers in industrialised countries to the working conditions experienced by people who make some of the goods that they purchase and consume. If globalisation is to work for poor people, governments, international institutions and civil society need to promote this awareness and support policies and regulatory systems that provide legal, physical and social protection for working people.

In 1998 the international community adopted the International Labour Organisation (ILO) Declaration on Fundamental Principles and Rights at Work. This Declaration covers the rights to freedom of association and to collective bargaining and the elimination of all forms of forced or compulsory labour, and of employment discrimination. The UK Government strongly supports this Declaration and we are working with the ILO and others to make progress towards the full realisation of these rights.

We are particularly committed to taking action against child labour. There are an estimated 250 million working children in developing countries. Most are trapped by the need to provide income for their desperately poor families. The UK has been a strong supporter of ILO Convention 182 on the Elimination of the Worst Forms of Child Labour. The UK ratified this Convention in March 2000 and is working with the ILO to achieve the widest possible ratification and implementation worldwide.

We are also supporting action internationally to strengthen the rights of workers in the informal sector, which is where the majority of poor people work, almost invariably in conditions unprotected by legislation or standards. The UK Government is helping contracted workers in the construction industries of Ghana, Zambia, India and Bangladesh to understand and realise their rights at work. Through Homenet, an international alliance of Trade Unions for homeworkers, we are helping women improve their market access and their legal and social protection.

And we are committed to promoting the core labour standards of poor people in formal employment. Through the Ethical Trading Initiative, for example, the UK Government is helping agricultural workers and their employers in the South African wine industry to improve labour standards.

PROMOTING EFFECTIVE GOVERNMENTS AND EFFICIENT MARKETS

79. The underlying causes of conflict differ, but societies will generally be less vulnerable to violence where economic and political systems are more inclusive – where all people have a stake in the economic, social and political systems of their countries. For example, the UK Government is working with others to help strengthen political institutions in the Palestinian Authority – in a region beset by economic, social and religious divisions.

80. Shortage of environmental resources can also be an important factor in conflict, both between and within countries. Tension and conflict can result where countries, or different groups within a country, compete for limited supplies of fresh water or other resources, or where environmental impacts such as climate change affect food policy or encourage migration. The UK Government, through its development strategies, will continue to promote inclusive development and equitable management of environmental resources.

81. Effective conflict prevention also requires a more joined-up approach to policy-making. The Government has established new arrangements to focus on conflict prevention, with pooled budgets and Joint Ministerial Committees to facilitate better working between different government departments. This will lead to better shared policy analysis, agreement on common policies and objectives, and the more flexible deployment of resources. The aim of these initiatives is to improve the UK Government's overall contribution to conflict prevention, reduction and management.

82. We are also committed to increasing our support for security sector reform. Unaccountable, ill-disciplined and repressive security forces are a major source of insecurity and human rights abuse. Security sectors that are badly managed can misappropriate resources that could be spent better on public services. A security sector that is appropriately tasked, managed and resourced, and subject to proper civilian oversight, can help to provide greater stability and security for poor people.

83. The international community also needs to regulate effectively the trade in arms. An estimated five million people have died in armed conflicts in the last decade – the vast majority of them civilians, and most of them killed by small arms.

84. The UK Government has taken a number of steps to tighten controls over arms exports. In 1997 the Government introduced new criteria for assessing licence applications for the export of arms and military equipment, in order to prevent the export of arms which might be used for internal repression or external aggression. And the UK was instrumental in getting agreement in 1998 to the establishment of an EU Code of Conduct on arms exports, which sets high common standards governing arms exports for all EU member states. It includes a

PROMOTING EFFECTIVE GOVERNMENTS AND EFFICIENT MARKETS

mechanism for discouraging countries from undercutting these standards. In September 2000, the UK Government also announced that it will introduce a licensing system to regulate the activities of arms brokers and traffickers[x].

85. In next year's UN Conference on small arms the UK Government will push for tighter international controls[3]. We will press for an action programme to include: more support for existing international, regional and national programmes to tackle small arms proliferation; efforts to ensure a common approach to the regulation of the legal transfer of small arms and light weapons; a commitment to work towards the effective regulation of arms brokers; and agreement to work towards the disposal and destruction of surplus weapons.

86. Many of the world's violent conflicts are fuelled by the trade in illicit drugs and high-value minerals. In order to break the vicious circle of conflict and illegal trade, more effort is required to deprive warlords of their ill-gotten gains.

87. The UK is working internationally to help build the capacity of law enforcement institutions to tackle the trade in illicit drugs, and to move this issue up the international agenda. We are hosting a G8 conference on the global economy of illegal drugs in 2001[4].

88. The Government's international development programme also has a role to play in tackling the threat from the global trade in illicit drugs[5]. In many developing countries and regions, poor households rely on the cultivation, production and trafficking of illicit drugs as sources of credit, income and employment. This requires policies to tackle the underlying reasons which encourage or force people to become involved in the drugs trade, for example alternative development programmes. It is also necessary to address why law enforcement organisations either tolerate or are unable effectively to combat the drugs trade.

89. We are also working to help producer countries to control better the mining and export of diamonds, in particular through prohibiting trade in uncertified diamonds from conflict regions[6].

Making markets work for the poor

90. The process of opening up – to both trade and financial flows – has to be carefully managed, to dovetail with the development of efficient and flexible markets, a strong domestic financial sector, and supportive policies for private investment. But the benefits will not automatically reach poor people, who face many barriers to participating in the market economy. While policies at the national and the international level play a vital role, the

---

[3] *UN Conference on the Illicit Trade in Small Arms and Light Weapons in All Its Aspects.*

[4] *The G7 Group of major industrialised democracies comprises Canada, France, Germany, Italy, Japan, the UK and the USA. The Group of Eight (G8) includes Russia. Their Heads of Government meet annually at the G7/G8 Summit to discuss areas of global concern.*

[5] *For a more detailed outline of the UK's policy see DFID Paper: Illicit Drugs and the Development Assistance Programme, DFID 1998.*

[6] *The international response to conflict is discussed further in Chapter 8.*

way in which government, institutions and markets function at the local level is of great importance too. Policy needs to work at all these levels if the potential benefits of globalisation are to reach the poor.

91. Poor people typically engage in a diverse range of economic activity in the formal and informal sectors: production, trade, selling their labour, and often migrating seasonally or longer term between rural and urban economies, in order to find the best opportunities for improving their livelihoods. They face a huge number of barriers to taking up these opportunities, ranging from lack of property rights, to limited access to credit and technology, poor infrastructure, and low skill levels, poor health and lack of adequate food and water.

92. Poor people, especially poor women, often lack land rights. Established property rights are needed not just for day-to-day security, but also to provide collateral against which people can borrow and invest. But these rights are often lacking. For example, in the Philippines, establishing legal ownership takes 168 steps and between 13-25 years. Being squatters rather than owners leaves people without the protection of the law, and security to borrow and invest. Land reform, providing secure access to land and other productive assets for poor people, whether through ownership, tenure or customary use rights,

is essential in building a market economy which will work for the poor.

93. Poor people in remote rural areas are often physically disconnected from market opportunities, through the absence or inadequacy of basic infrastructure such as rural roads, electricity and telecommunications. An evaluation of the UK's support for investment in rural roads in Mozambique showed that building dirt roads led to increased agricultural production because crops could be transferred to market. It also improved access to education and health care.

94. Opening up the provision of financial and information services can bring major benefits. Access to credit is a particular problem for women and minority communities. Special measures are frequently needed to help micro-enterprises and small business. These are the main source of employment in developing countries, yet these companies are often acutely exposed to bureaucratic harassment, capricious and inappropriate regulations, and the buying of privilege by the well-connected.

95. Poor people, with no assets or savings to fall back on, are also particularly vulnerable in times of economic change. Good social policies are needed to help poor people to cope with change and to take advantage of its opportunities. These are likely to combine state supported actions (ranging from public works and stay-in-school programmes), with effective regulation (for example of banks, pension funds or social insurance schemes), and a range of activities of non-governmental organisations (including faith organisations and charities).

96. The UK Government believes that good social policy goes together with good economic policy: investment in social services and social protection is an essential investment in economic development. Through our development partnerships and within the multilateral institutions, we will promote inclusive social policies that protect those who may lose from rapid economic change, and policies to equip people to benefit from new opportunities.

THE UK GOVERNMENT WILL:

- Work to promote effective systems of government and efficient markets in developing countries.

- Promote political reform including support for inclusive, accountable and representative systems of government which respect the human rights of the poor.

- Help to tackle corruption, including through legislation to give UK courts jurisdiction over UK nationals who commit offences of corruption abroad, tightening the law on money laundering, permitting the restraint of assets at an earlier stage in the investigative process and strengthening the arrangements which give overseas governments access to the courts and investigative authorities in the UK.

- Work with developing countries and local communities to address the problem of child labour.

- Strengthen its commitment to conflict prevention through our new Africa and Global Conflict Prevention Initiatives.

- Support effective security sector reform, to ensure that security sectors are appropriately structured and managed and subject to proper civilian control.

- Introduce a licensing system to control UK arms brokers and traffickers, and work for tighter controls internationally at next year's UN conference on small arms.

A more detailed account of the UK Government's policies on human rights, effective governance, and women is set out in three DFID Strategy Papers: 'Human rights for poor people', 'Making Government work for poor people', and 'Poverty elimination and the empowerment of women', and in a separate policy statement on 'Poverty and the Security Sector'.

Investing in People, Sharing Skills and Knowledge

The UK Government will:

- **Promote better health and education for poor people, and harness the new information and communications technologies to share skills and knowledge with developing countries.**

- **Help focus more of the UK and global research effort on the needs of the poor, and make intellectual property regimes work better for poor people.**

Promoting better health for poor people

97. Poor people suffer disproportionately from poor health and malnutrition. The poorest 20 per cent of the global population have a 14-fold higher risk of death in childhood than the richest 20 per cent. Similarly, more women die from pregnancy in India in a week than in the whole of Europe in a year.

98. Better health is essential if poor people and countries are to benefit from globalisation. For individual families, better health means less suffering and less time and expense invested in caring for ill family members, improved physical and intellectual development, enhanced school attendance and learning, and higher productivity at work. For countries, better health is now accepted as a central long-term driver of economic growth. For example, it has been estimated that controlling malaria in those parts of Africa where it is endemic would raise Gross Domestic Product by 20 per cent over a fifteen year period[xi].

99. Globalisation has had a number of major health effects, as people, money and goods have become more mobile. The increased movement of people seeking employment; urbanisation; changes in behaviour and the wider availability of illicit drugs have led to the more rapid transmission of diseases like malaria, HIV/AIDS, and Tuberculosis (TB). TB kills more than 2 million people each year, malaria more than a million. More than 36 million people worldwide are infected with HIV.

100. Increased migration, whether for economic or political reasons, conflict or natural disasters, has also caused health problems arising from the loss of traditional safety nets and the adaptation to new environments. Displaced populations tend to be particularly vulnerable to communicable diseases such as malaria, meningitis, pneumonia and diarrhoea. Conflict and rapid population movement is also associated with an increase in sexually transmitted diseases, in particular HIV/AIDS. And changing consumption patterns are leading to an increase in non-communicable disease. Based on current trends, 70 per cent of tobacco-related deaths will be in developing countries by

BOX 4

THE IMPACT OF HIV/AIDS[xii]

HIV/AIDS is both a human and a development tragedy. Around 22 million people have died of AIDS, with 16,000 new HIV infections every day. More than 90 per cent of the infections are in the developing world, with nearly 70 per cent in sub-Saharan Africa. In India over 3 million adults have HIV/AIDS, and in Cambodia, Thailand and Burma over 2 per cent of the adult population is estimated to be infected.

In a number of sub-Saharan African countries, average life expectancy has fallen by 20 years. The cost of treatment and care for people living with HIV/AIDS impoverishes many families and communities. The need for care forces potential wage earners to stay at home, young girls to miss school, changes to agricultural practice which reduce nutritional value, and leads to valuable family assets being sold to pay for treatment. Within the next five years there could be as many as 40 million maternal orphans as a result of HIV/AIDS, children with reduced likelihood of attaining good health and having a good education.

The cost to the economy of HIV/AIDS is also massive. Health budgets have to be increased, at the expense of other sectors. Government finance comes under pressure as expenditure increases and tax revenues decrease. Death and absenteeism reduce labour supply and productivity. In the worst-hit countries the workforce is likely to be more than 17 per cent smaller in 2015 than it would have been without AIDS. Zambia, for example, lost 1,300 teachers from AIDS in the first 10 months of 1998, more than two-thirds of the number of all new teachers trained that year. And economic growth is weaker. For the 16 countries in eastern, central and southern Africa with HIV infection rates above 10 per cent of adults, GDP growth will be at least 1 per cent a year lower. One estimate for South Africa is that overall GDP will be 17 per cent lower in 2010, and GDP per capita 7 per cent lower.

2030. The UK will support developing countries' efforts to develop tobacco control strategies within the World Health Organisation (WHO) Framework Convention.

101. Globalisation has also created international markets for health. Not only do people travel overseas for their healthcare – health personnel do the same in search of jobs. In some cases, such as Bangladesh, this has been an explicit policy. In others it has contributed significantly to brain drain – there are about a third as many Ugandan doctors in South Africa as in Uganda.

102. The UK Government is committed to working to meet the International Development Targets for health. And we work closely with developing country governments and key international institutions, including the WHO, UNAIDS, the United Nations Population Fund, the World Bank and the European Commission. We have recently agreed a further £35 million of support for WHO work on polio eradication. This is part of an internationally agreed strategy, led by WHO, to eradicate polio within five years.

103. The UK Government is working to strengthen the international effort to combat the diseases of the poor, with a greater focus on communicable diseases, including the development of new drugs and vaccines to help tackle these. The effectiveness of this effort depends critically on basic health care systems at the national level, drawing on the resources of both the public and private sectors. We need to ensure not only that affordable drugs and vaccines are available, but also that there are effective systems to deliver these to all who need them. Strong national leadership is essential if these health care systems are to be put in place.

Spreading educational opportunity

104. Education and skills are the commanding heights of the modern global economy. Globalisation – and the growth of knowledge-based systems of production – is both increasing the rewards for education and raising the costs of exclusion from it. If globalisation is to work for poor people, increased investment in education, lifelong learning and skills is essential.

105. One of the ways in which globalisation could help to eliminate poverty is by speeding up the diffusion of knowledge and technology to developing countries. But for countries to make use of

modern technology, they must improve education and skills training.

106. And that starts at the primary level. Where countries invest in high-quality primary education for all – particularly for girls – the development dividends are enormous. Education of girls is probably the single most effective investment in development that any country can make.

107. But huge numbers of children today – girls and boys – do not take even this initial step. An estimated 113 million children of primary-school age have never gone to school (see figure 3.1). Around 150 million children have dropped out after a few years, still unable to read, write or work with numbers. And one in four adults in the developing world – that is 870 million people – are unable to read or write[xiii].

108. It is for this reason that, over the last three and half years, the UK Government has greatly strengthened its commitment to education, particularly at the basic and primary level. Since our last White Paper in 1997 we have committed over £400 million to support the development of primary education systems.

109. We now have total education commitments of £800 million, with nearly 80 per cent of these resources allocated to basic and primary education sectors. We

INVESTING IN PEOPLE, SHARING SKILLS AND KNOWLEDGE

FIGURE 3.1

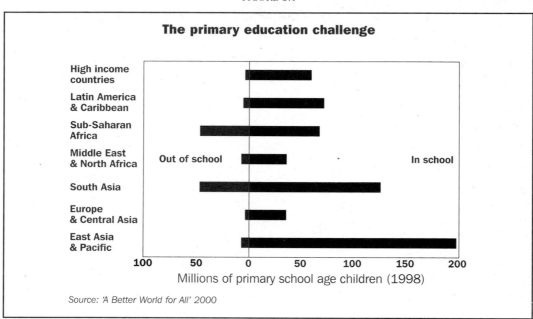

The primary education challenge

High income countries

Latin America & Caribbean

Sub-Saharan Africa

Middle East & North Africa   Out of school   In school

South Asia

Europe & Central Asia

East Asia & Pacific

100   50   0   50   100   150   200

Millions of primary school age children (1998)

Source: 'A Better World for All' 2000

have focused these extra resources on the poorest countries in Africa and south Asia, the regions with the worst education indicators.

110. And we are spending that money in new ways – working with governments to develop well-integrated and sustainable education systems, helping them to provide high-quality primary education to all their children. These sector-wide education partnerships are characteristic of our work in countries such as Uganda, South Africa, Ghana, Malawi, Rwanda, China, Vietnam, and in the states of West Bengal and Andhra Pradesh in India.

111. This focus on the sector as a whole recognises that countries need a balanced approach to the expansion of education. Success in improving access and quality at the primary education level leads to increased demand for post-primary education and for teacher training. This in turn requires improvements in higher education. Jobs, whether in the modern manufacturing or service sectors, increasingly have a strong information processing and knowledge content. East Asia's experience shows that sustained export-led growth, and the development of the learning economy, require the investment in secondary and tertiary education essential to enhance capacity to research, analyse, train and manage.

112. New technologies are offering new ways to improve the supply of education, particularly through the use of distance learning. The UK Government is working with the Commonwealth of Learning to encourage the development of distance learning. And through the Prime Minister's education initiative (see box 5), we are

BOX 5

THE PRIME MINISTER'S INITIATIVE

The Prime Minister's initiative on technology in teacher training, known as 'Imfundo' (Ndebele for education), is a new kind of public/private partnership dedicated to finding new ways to enhance educational opportunity in developing countries, with a particular focus on sub-Saharan Africa. The initiative has been developed in partnership with Cisco, Marconi and Virgin.

Imfundo will use information and communication technologies such as radio, satellite, computers and the internet to support teacher training, professional development and support, and the management of education systems.

Through the initiative, resource centres can be established in district centres to which teachers can travel periodically. These centres will provide access to a wide range of resources, including printed materials, audio, video and the Internet. This will enable trainees to interact with their tutors and with each other.

Distance learning of this kind permits developing countries to train many more teachers to a much higher standard than would be possible by conventional means. At the same time, teachers can learn new skills and become familiar with computers and the Internet, increasing their status and bringing wider benefits to the community.

exploring new opportunities for using distance learning and information technology for teacher training and the sharing of skills and knowledge, with a particular focus on Africa.

113. But our priority focus remains effective investment in primary schooling. The UK Government is committed to driving forward the agenda of the 2000 World Education Forum in Dakar, Senegal. At this meeting, governments, international institutions and civil society reaffirmed their commitment to the two core International Development Targets on education – universal primary education by 2015, and gender equality in primary and secondary schooling by 2005. The Dakar Framework for Action commits countries

to develop or strengthen their own national plans of action by 2002.

114. Dakar also affirmed that *'no countries seriously committed to Education for All will be thwarted in their achievement of this goal by lack of resources'*. The UK Government will act in support of that aim, working with other development agencies to increase support for countries with a clear commitment to universal primary education. We will work with international institutions and developing countries to make faster progress towards the education development targets.

115. No child should be denied access to a basic education because she or he, their parents or guardians cannot pay for it.

Even when education is nominally free, some direct costs are often passed on in the form of charges for books, uniforms, exams and transport. These direct costs can reach up to 20 per cent of a family's income, making it unaffordable to many. The UK Government will continue to work to improve poor people's access to education.

Bridging the digital divide

116. New technologies have slashed the cost of processing, storing and moving information. They have the potential to help poor people leapfrog some of the traditional barriers to development, by linking them into the global economy, improving their access to knowledge and making government machinery work better[xiv, xv].

FIGURE 3.2

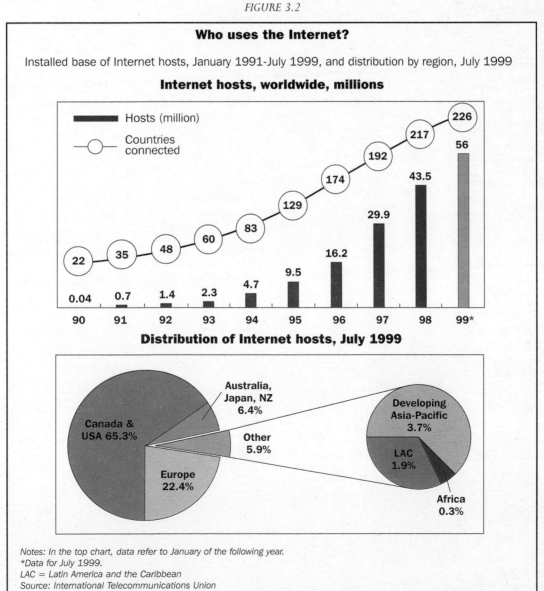

Who uses the Internet?

Installed base of Internet hosts, January 1991-July 1999, and distribution by region, July 1999

Internet hosts, worldwide, millions

Hosts (million)
Countries connected

	90	91	92	93	94	95	96	97	98	99*
Hosts	0.04	0.7	1.4	2.3	4.7	9.5	16.2	29.9	43.5	56
Countries	22	35	48	60	83	129	174	192	217	226

Distribution of Internet hosts, July 1999

Canada & USA 65.3%
Europe 22.4%
Australia, Japan, NZ 6.4%
Other 5.9%
Developing Asia-Pacific 3.7%
LAC 1.9%
Africa 0.3%

Notes: In the top chart, data refer to January of the following year.
*Data for July 1999.
LAC = Latin America and the Caribbean
Source: International Telecommunications Union

117. The Internet and mobile telephones offer poor countries new things to sell – from basic data entry to software – and new ways of selling old products, by cutting out the middlemen. They can also help attract investment to poor countries and enable people to communicate with each other more freely and efficiently, both nationally and internationally.

118. But there is a real risk that poor countries and poor people will be marginalised, that the existing educational divide will be compounded by a growing digital divide (see figure 3.2). Watching the staggering growth of new technologies in the developed world, it is easy to forget that more than half the people in Africa have never used a phone. It is not that access is physically impossible. You can surf the Internet in almost every country in the world. But in many developing countries, particularly in Africa, logging on is more expensive than in developed countries.

119. A key constraint on Internet access in most developing countries is the lack of a legal and regulatory framework for a competitive telecommunications sector. Without this, there is no hope of attracting the necessary investment in infrastructure or encouraging the competition needed to bring down costs. Governments need to move from state-run telecoms monopolies, with administered prices, to a regulatory environment which allows competition,

including over international routes, and to cut tariffs on imported hardware. But the reforms necessarily present difficult challenges in the short-term, requiring governments to forego significant sources of revenue. The International Financial Institutions have a key role to play in working with developing countries in smoothing this adjustment process.

120 Some developing countries have been concerned that Internet backbone companies (the infrastructure which carries Internet traffic) will not interconnect with their Internet Service Providers (ISPs) on a no-charge basis; instead their ISPs have to pay the costs of interconnection and of the international leased line. At the International Telecommunications Union World Telecommunication Standardisation Assembly in October 2000, the UK helped to achieve agreement by developing and developed countries to a statement of the principles which should underpin future commercial negotiations in this area.

121. We are also keen to see developing countries become more fully involved in the negotiations on communications related agreements in the World Trade Organisation (WTO) and for them to play a greater role in other international organisations which have an impact on Information and Communications Technology (ICT) policy. Poor countries are currently on the sidelines of the global information economy and it is important that the international community agrees policies and standards that encourage rather than act as a barrier to their entry.

122. But if they want to make the most of the new technologies, developing countries need to look inwards as well as outwards. There is a risk that richer people in cities will get increasingly connected, while their poorer fellow-citizens are increasingly marginalised. Communal access programmes are one way of reducing that risk. Combining new technologies with communal access models or pay as you go schemes means that access can become economic, even in remote rural areas. In Bangladesh, for example, there is a scheme through which poor people can get a loan to buy a mobile phone and set up a tiny telecentre. The scheme has proved highly successful: the loans have been paid back and remote communities have access.

123. Access can also be broadened by combining new technologies with the old. For example, although less than one in a thousand Africans currently has access to the Internet, radio has wide penetration, even into the remotest of villages. A growing number of community radio stations are getting connected to the Internet, allowing new material to be shared with much larger audiences.

124. Developing countries also need to raise skill levels and to develop locally relevant applications and content, including in local languages. We believe public-private partnerships have a key role to play in mobilising the resources to do this. We welcome the increasing focus by multinationals on training information and technology professionals in developing countries, and we are keen to work with them – for example on trade and investment promotion packages, and teacher training materials. The Commonwealth Business Council, for example, has developed a gateway (CBCmarketplace.com), which they hope will lead to increased e-commerce within developing countries in the Commonwealth.

125. We believe new technologies can play an important role in improving education in developing countries, from primary through to the tertiary level. There is also growing interest in the way they can improve public sector performance. The state of Andhra Pradesh in India, for instance, is using new technologies effectively in its health care, education and poverty reduction programmes and to improve its tax collection.

126. The world is at a critical juncture in the development of ICT with a number of different technologies (e.g. mobile telephones, the Internet, and digital) coming together and with costs falling.

This is changing fundamentally the way business is conducted. For poorer developing countries - faced with urgent health and education priorities - this might not seem immediately relevant. But the constraints on access to ICT for developing countries are in the first instance regulatory, and can and should be addressed alongside investments in education and health. The international community must also play its part through ensuring that international agreements are supportive, and in helping to address revenue shortfalls as the telecommunications sector adjusts to a more open and competitive environment.

Re-thinking the mobility of people

127. Globalisation also requires us to re-think our approach to the mobility of people. The spread of ideas and technical know-how lies at the heart of successful development. The development of modern communication technology has made this easier and cheaper. And quicker and easier transport has made it possible for those with expertise to move around the world, living in one country but working in others.

128. Transnational companies and long-term supply contracts both provide important channels for the transfer of knowledge. For example, foreign buyers provide technical assistance in design, production and packaging to firms in Indonesia producing shoes and clothes for the US market, and advice on crop selection, growing and logistics to farms in Kenya producing vegetables for European supermarkets.

129. Government policies in developing countries should promote the mobility that will make this sharing of know-how possible. Good airports and tele-communications are vital – and if the poor are to benefit, there must be easy access to many parts of the country, not just to one or two large cities. Simple measures to reduce delays and difficulties – in customs and immigration procedures, or in approving contracts and projects – and action to improve personal security, can also yield large benefits.

130. Trade in services has become increasingly important in the global economy. The General Agreement on Trade in Services identifies the temporary movement of people to another country – in order to provide the service there – as one of the ways in which trade in services takes place (this is defined in the Agreement as the 'movement of natural persons').

131. Developing countries are particularly concerned that regulations governing the temporary entry, stay and working conditions of their nationals should not unfairly restrict their ability to sell services into developed country markets. The current negotiations on services in the WTO offer an opportunity for all countries to move forward in ensuring that such regulations do not unnecessarily restrict trade in services, and are applied in a transparent, consistent and non-discriminatory way.

132. A further feature of globalisation has been intense global competition for people with scarce skills in areas such as information technology and the health sector. Developed countries are responding to shortages of health personnel by actively recruiting skilled staff from low and middle income countries.

133. There are benefits to individuals – in terms of career opportunities and earnings – as well as to the health or information and technology sectors of developed countries. For developing countries, these outflows of skilled people generate significant remittances. Longer-term benefits may include the new skills and contacts brought back by returning migrants. But these outflows can also be a drain on human resources in critically short supply[xvi]. We are undertaking more research on this issue.

134. The UK believes that developed countries need to be more sensitive to the impact on developing countries of a skills

drain. They need to ensure that policies in this area do not unfairly restrict the ability of developing country service suppliers to sell into their markets, yet also do not worsen skill shortages in developing countries. In line with this principle, the National Health Service has developed a set of ethical guidelines which rule out recruitment from a particular country if this has a negative effect on that country's healthcare services.

Encouraging pro-poor research

135. Most research and development capacity is in developed countries and is oriented to their needs. Research that benefits the poor is an example of a global public good which is underfunded. Not enough of the world's knowledge is relevant for the needs of the poor. For instance, 90 per cent of the world's disease burden is the subject of less than 10 per cent of all international research on health[xvii].

136. More and more research is done in the private sector, and the low purchasing power of poor people means that there is little commercial incentive to invest in research to meet their needs. Governments and development agencies must therefore work to create more partnerships and must also invest directly and substantially in research that benefits poor people.

137. In agriculture, because most enterprises are too small to do research, publicly funded research remains important. The work of the Consultative Group on International Agricultural Research is vital. It is essential that it moves forward with reforms to its governance, organisation and structure so that it can deal with the increasing complexities of its role in public goods research and in the organisation and management of genetic resources and intellectual property. Efforts must also be made to strengthen the capability of developing countries to produce, adapt and use knowledge, whether produced locally or internationally.

138. In health, innovative partnerships between public agencies, foundations and private sector companies are tackling globally important diseases by creating programmes to develop and test new international public goods, such as the International Aids Vaccine Initiative and the Medicines for Malaria Venture.

139. Promising new ideas are also under discussion, such as public purchase funds to help develop new vaccines against HIV/AIDS, malaria or TB. Under such a scheme, governments would guarantee to buy vaccines for developing country markets, at a fixed price, from any firm that could develop an effective new product, thus providing the private sector with the financial incentive that is now missing. The expenditure would be incurred if, and only if, a successful product was developed.

140. Other proposals aimed at developing incentive frameworks are under discussion. These include differential pricing – selling drugs and vaccines at a lower price in developing countries than in developed countries; extending the period of intellectual property protection, allowing companies exclusive rights to market drugs and vaccines over a longer period, at a more affordable price; and the use of tax credits.

141. The UK Government has commissioned urgent work to develop new proposals to tackle the lack of incentives for, and the perceived risks of, increased investment in research into vaccines and treatments to tackle HIV/AIDS, malaria and TB. This will look at the full range of possibilities. We will decide on possible financial support in light of the findings of this work. We will also share these findings in full with WHO, as well as with our EU partners, and with other members of the G7/G8 as part of the preparations for the Summit in 2001[xviii].

Intellectual property regimes and developing countries

142. Intellectual property rights (IPR) – for instance, conferring copyright, patent or trade mark protection – provide an essential incentive for private investment in research and development. This is particularly so in medicine and agriculture, where research can be costly and long-term, and where the results are uncertain.

143. Developing countries have an important interest in providing intellectual property protection, as a way of encouraging more investment, research and innovation from which they should benefit. The precise details of IPR regimes need to be tailored to the particular circumstances of individual countries. The WTO Agreement on Trade-Related Aspects of Intellectual Property Rights (TRIPs) sets out minimum standards of intellectual property protection. The UK Government believes that the agreement allows WTO members sufficient flexibility to implement domestic IPR regimes which take adequate account of their national circumstances.

144. One concern in this area has been that patenting regimes will restrict the availability or increase the cost of essential drugs, seeds or technological process, and thereby reduce poor people's access to them. A key issue here is the extent to which national IPR regimes permit the importing of goods from the cheapest legitimate international source. The TRIPs agreement does not prevent governments from doing this, and there are no proposals from TRIPs signatories to restrict this flexibility. The agreement also allows for

the possibility of 'compulsory licensing' in exceptional circumstances, where efforts to reach agreement between the right-holder and the user have been unsuccesful.[7]

145. At the same time, we recognise that some developing countries face real difficulties in implementing the agreement on time, that some have concerns about its impact, and that some would like to see changes to the Agreement. For this reason, we support extending deadlines in cases where countries are committed to implementing the agreement but have genuine difficulties in doing so within current deadlines. We are ready to help countries to develop and implement IPR regimes suited to their national circumstances. We are committed to monitoring the impact of TRIPs, including on poor people's access to vital drugs. And we are open to constructive suggestions on how to improve the agreement in TRIPs reviews and to more substantive negotiations in the context of a new Trade Round.

146. The TRIPs agreement does not cover traditional knowledge or access to indigenous genetic resources, and there have been some concerns that developing countries are losing potential benefits as a result. The World Intellectual Property Organisation is currently examining options for the protection of rights to indigenous knowledge. Mechanisms for access to genetic resources are being further

---

[7]   *Compulsory licensing is a mechanism which enables national governments to licence a patented product to be produced domestically by a manufacturer other than the patent holder.*

developed under the Convention on Biological Diversity and the International Undertaking on Plant Genetic Resources for Food and Agriculture.

147. We support the development of internationally recognised standards, consistent with the objectives of intellectual property agreements, for the protection of traditional knowledge and access to genetic resources, which will help ensure fair and equitable benefit-sharing from their use. We also recognise the need to ensure that intellectual property agreements accommodate and support these standards as they are developed and that such agreements, including TRIPs and the Convention on Biological Diversity, continue to be implemented in a mutually supportive manner.

148. Another concern in this area has been that transnational companies may be able to patent the results of research which should be made freely available as an 'global public good', for instance the human genome, or plant and animal genomes. We are committed to working for international agreement on the need to release fundamental information on the human genome and the DNA sequences of the world's major naturally occurring food crop and livestock species into the public domain.

149. Given the complexities of these issues, the UK Government will establish a Commission (see Box 6), chaired by an eminent person, and including a representative group of international figures, to look at the ways that intellectual property rules need to develop in the future in order to take greater account of the interests of developing countries and poor people. This will report to the Secretary of State for International Development.

BOX 6

COMMISSION ON INTELLECTUAL PROPERTY RIGHTS (IPR)

The Commission will consider:

(i) how national IPR regimes should best be designed to benefit developing countries within the context of international agreements, including TRIPS;

(ii) how the international framework of rules and agreements might be improved and developed - for instance in the area of traditional knowledge – and the relationship between IPR rules and regimes covering access to genetic resources;

(iii) the broader policy framework needed to complement intellectual property regimes, including for instance controlling anti-competitive practices through competition policy and law.

INVESTING IN PEOPLE, SHARING SKILLS AND KNOWLEDGE

THE UK GOVERNMENT WILL:

- Work to strengthen the international effort to tackle the diseases of poverty including HIV/AIDS, TB, malaria and childhood infectious disease.

- Work to ensure that primary education is free for all, that no government seriously committed to universal primary education is unable to achieve this for lack of resources, and work with international institutions and developing countries to make faster progress towards the education targets.

- Support, where appropriate, the use of new technologies to help with teacher training and the sharing of skills.

- Work to ensure that a development perspective is included in international agreements affecting telecommunications and new technologies, and for a stronger voice for poorer countries in setting these rules in international institutions.

- Seek to ensure that the entry and work permit rules and other policies of developed countries do not unfairly restrict the ability of developing country service suppliers to sell into developing country markets, whilst also taking into account the need not to worsen skill shortages in developing countries.

- Seek to increase public and private sector research for development, including through new mechanisms to tackle the current lack of incentives for research into vaccines and treatments for HIV/AIDS, Malaria and TB.

- Establish a Commission, chaired by an eminent person, to look at how intellectual property rules might need to develop in the future to take greater account of the interests of developing countries and poor people.

A more detailed account of the UK Government's policies on Health and Education are set out in two DFID Strategy Papers: 'Better health for poor people', and 'Education for all - the challenge of Universal Primary Education'.

HARNESSING PRIVATE FINANCE

> *The UK Government will:*
>
> - Work with developing countries to put in place conditions that will attract private financial flows and minimise the risk of capital flight.
>
> - Work to strengthen the global financial system to manage the risks associated with the scale, speed and volatility of global financial flows, including through use of 'road maps' to guide countries on opening of their capital accounts.
>
> - Encourage international co-operation on investment, competition and tax that promotes the interests of developing countries.
>
> - Encourage corporate social responsibility by national and transnational companies, and more investment by them in developing countries.

The pattern of capital flows

150. A central feature of globalisation has been the substantial increase in movement of capital around the world. Foreign direct investment (FDI) to developing countries increased from US$36 billion in 1992 to US$155 billion in 1999, more than three times the level of development aid. But the pattern of these flows is heavily skewed towards the larger and more industrialised of the developing countries[xix].

151. This picture is not so stark when the relative size of the economies of developed and developing countries is taken into account. As a proportion of their national wealth, developing countries receive more FDI than do developed countries. But there is no room for complacency – many developing countries need access to foreign finance because their own savings rates are very low.

152. In addition to FDI, developing countries have also gained access to international capital markets in the past decade. The purchase of bonds and equities issued by governments and firms in developing countries increased from US$63 billion in 1992 to a peak of US$105 billion in 1994. These 'portfolio flows' fell back to only US$5 billion in 1999 following the East Asian financial crisis. The reversal was even more dramatic in the case of short-term bank lending with a peak inflow of US$75 billion in 1995 turning into an outflow of US$91 billion in 1999. Such volatility is very damaging for economic development and poverty reduction.

153. In many developing countries a considerable part of private wealth is held abroad rather than contributing to national development. The reasons for this include domestic conflict, tax evasion and political

FIGURE 4.1

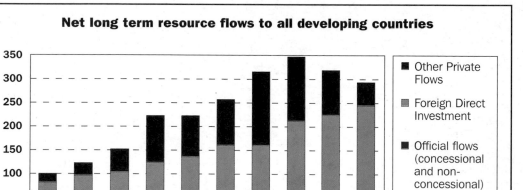

Note: Other Private Flows consists predominately of Portfolio Flows and Bank lending (see paragraph 152).
Source:IMF World Economic Outlook 2000

corruption: it is estimated that 40 per cent of African private wealth is held overseas compared with only 4 per cent in Asia[xx]. In some cases, the problem is partly due to poor economic controls. In Russia, capital flight has fallen dramatically from around $25 billion in 1998 to $15 billion in 1999 as a result of tightening economic controls[xxi]. Where investment conditions in a country markedly improve some of this capital can be attracted back. For example in Uganda – following an economic reform and stabilisation programme – net private capital inflows more than doubled as a percentage of Gross National Product (GNP).

Supporting sound domestic policies

154. The attraction of capital inflows is an essential element of a strategy to speed up sustainable development and poverty reduction. But only a small proportion of external flows are invested directly in the micro and small enterprise sector, which are the main source of new jobs and incomes for the poor.

155. It is essential therefore that reforms to attract financial flows be complemented by other reforms which ensure that external financial services are available to the poor. These services range from simple community-based savings instruments, credit and insurance for micro-enterprises, to an efficient banking system that serves all registered businesses.

156. Foreign investment does not substitute for domestic investment but it can complement it. The challenge is to maximise the benefits of increased foreign investment, including that from transnational corporations, by creating strong links to the domestic economy (see box 7). Such measures include financial sector reform, strengthened competition and tax policy, a careful approach to capital account liberalisation and responsible behaviour by investors themselves.

157. For capital flows to be stable and productive, developing countries need to put in place improved domestic policies. And the conditions that attract foreign investment are the same conditions that generate domestic savings, promote domestic investment, and discourage capital flight. They include: an economic and political environment that is stable and predictable, supported by transparent laws, fair competition and reliable legal systems; and the reduction of administrative barriers to investment. In Mozambique for example – a country which has undertaken such reform – there has been a six-fold increase in FDI since 1994.

158. An improved investment pattern requires a strong competition policy if it is to be sustainable. This is essential to ensure that large companies, whether local or international, do not exploit monopoly

BOX 7

TRANSNATIONAL CORPORATIONS

Transnational Corporations (TNCs) are an important part of the process of globalisation. There are now some 63,000 TNC parent firms with around 690,000 foreign affiliates. The foreign affiliates of the top 100 TNCs have assets of the order of $2 trillion. Sales by foreign affiliates worldwide are now twice as large as global exports. Most TNCs are large companies based in developed countries but they include a growing number of firms from developing and transition economies and small and medium-sized firms. The huge expansion of international production has been facilitated by countries world-wide, including developing and transition countries, adopting more favourable policies towards foreign investors.

TNCs can contribute significantly to economic development in host countries through their technology, specialised skills and ability to organise and integrate production across countries, to establish marketing networks and to access finance and equipment on favourable terms.

To reap these benefits developing countries need to encourage links to the domestic economy, including linkages with domestic suppliers and subcontractors, and to promote the capacity and skills to make good use of these links. TNCs should also be subject to adequate regulation: in a world of international production, domestic policies on finance, investment, competition and taxation need to be designed and integrated within an international framework of rules. And this needs to be matched by TNCs themselves adhering to high standards of corporate social responsibility, including through the revised OECD Guidelines for Multinational Enterprises.

Source: UNCTAD World Investment Report 2000.

---

power and indulge in restrictive business practices – such as market quotas and price fixing. Such practices harm consumers and constrain the growth of the small firms that create employment. Competition policy thus needs to be complemented by measures that address the needs of small enterprises, such as the provision of skills and technology, access to investment and finance, and support to increase sales in national and international markets.

159. Domestic tax policy is crucial. In recent years, many developing countries have offered investment subsidies, including tax incentives, to attract transnational firms. Such subsidies are intended to generate new employment. But in practice they often fail to alter the investment decisions of firms, and merely erode a country's tax base. In some cases such tax incentives have given perverse incentives for unsustainable and inefficient exploitation of natural resources such as water, forests and fisheries. The experience of Uganda and other countries suggests that simplification of a country's tax regime may be a more effective way to encourage companies to invest.

160. The pursuit of policies that encourage investment also has implications for a country's approach to the regulation of direct investment and controls on short-term capital flows. Capital controls take many forms, including outright prohibitions on certain types of foreign investment, as well as quantitative restrictions on financial flows. These controls can act as a barrier to foreign investment, particularly if they discriminate against foreign investors.

161. It is for this reason that, until recently, the international financial institutions were pushing countries to remove these controls, and to remove them quickly. However recent experience – not least the Asian financial crisis – has shown that the sequencing of liberalisation with reform is crucial. It has also shown that there are risks associated with rapid capital account liberalisation, in advance of a well functioning macro-economy, open and transparent policy-making and effective financial regulation.

162. The UK Government favours a more country-specific approach to capital controls, and a gradual approach to the opening up of capital accounts. An important part of this is to work with countries and international institutions to design 'road maps' for the opening up of capital accounts.

163. Such maps should offer guidance on the speed of liberalisation, and on the appropriate reforms needed to make it a success. Practical programmes of advice and assistance must help countries to strengthen the financial sector, including through enhanced banking supervision, stronger bankruptcy laws and property rights, an independent judicial system, and the use of private sector finance and skills.

164. In countries which have weak financial sectors and are at the earlier stages of liberalisation, there may sometimes be a case for specific measures to help to discourage excessive short-term capital inflows, whilst encouraging longer-term flows. However such measures should be viewed as a temporary means of facilitating the reforms needed to ensure orderly and sustainable liberalisation.

Strengthening the international financial system

165. While national governments have the primary responsibility for putting in place policies that encourage domestic and foreign investment, the international institutions and exporters of capital also have important responsibilities. Greater integration into global financial markets exposes developing countries to external shocks. And these shocks can lead to economic downturns and increased poverty.

166. The responsibility on the international financial institutions – the International Monetary Fund (IMF) and World Bank in particular, but also the larger OECD countries – is therefore to help manage the global economy in a way that reduces these risks and promotes

economic stability, sustainable growth and development.

167. The focus of the World Bank is poverty reduction, structural reform and social development[8]. To that end it acts as a key intermediary between the capital markets of developed countries and developing country borrowers who would not otherwise have access to those markets. The IMF has a central role in promoting international financial stability and in contributing to the establishment of sound macro-economic and financial policies, helping countries to access private capital flows.

168. The UK Government believes that both the IMF and the World Bank have an important role to play in promoting pro-poor economic growth and integration of developing economies into global markets. We do not agree with those who argue that the IMF's role in low income countries should pass to the World Bank. The IMF is uniquely placed to offer the technical advice and support for countries to maintain the macro-economic foundations required for successful growth and poverty reduction.

169. We also believe there is an important role for IMF medium-term lending in middle income countries in order to tackle deep-rooted structural reform. But we believe that IMF

---

[8] *The World Bank is discussed further in Chapter 7.*

programmes should take better account of their impact on the lives of the poor.

170. We welcome the fact that the World Bank and the IMF have now endorsed the International Development Targets and that, in low income countries, the IMF's new Poverty Reduction and Growth Facility must now derive from a country's own Poverty Reduction Strategy[9]. In both low and middle income countries it is important that the World Bank and IMF work together more effectively and seek better structures for cooperation. The recent joint statement by the World Bank President and IMF Managing Director promising an enhanced partnership between the two institutions is a good starting point.

171. We will encourage the IMF to take greater account of the relationship between stabilisation, structural issues, poverty and growth in programme design in low and middle income countries. The two institutions should also support open and broad debate within countries about the design of their policies, and encourage independent assessment of the impact of these policies on the poor and on the environment.

172. But even with stronger domestic policies, there is still a threat of financial instability. The UK Government is working for further reforms in the way the international system operates. It needs to be strengthened to spot potential problems early, to prevent these problems where possible and to minimise the disruption and damage they can cause.

173. First, we need improved surveillance – better monitoring of the performance of developed and developing country economies, and greater transparency in this process. The timely availability of accurate data to investors should help to avoid sudden shocks and outflows of investors' funds.

174. Over the past two years the international community has made progress in agreeing a framework of codes and standards needed for successful participation in global capital markets. These cover data dissemination requirements, transparency in fiscal and monetary policy, financial supervision and corporate governance.

175. But these codes and standards will only work if there is an effective surveillance mechanism to monitor their implementation, so that the public and investors are well informed and can have confidence in the information provided. We believe that an enhanced IMF surveillance process (through their Article IV reviews), which draws on the work and expertise of others, provides the best framework.

176. Adopting these standards in countries at widely different levels of

---

[9]   For more on Poverty Reduction Strategies see Chapter 7.

development requires careful consideration of sequencing and timing. Provision of technical assistance is crucial to ensure that developing countries are not left behind in this process. There are particular challenges for the poorest and small economies where banking systems are weak, domestic budgets still rely heavily on development assistance, and capital markets are almost non-existent. The UK Government is committed to establishing a new technical assistance facility to help take this work forward.

177. Second, there needs to be a strengthening of the international system's approach to crisis resolution. There will continue to be a role for the IMF in resolving crisis, but given the sheer size of private flows, private sector lenders must expect to play a part.

178. National governments can also take steps to facilitate orderly crisis resolution by forging regular and lasting contacts with their private investors, establishing overdraft facilities with international banks (to provide finance in an emergency), and making use of collective action bond clauses[10]. The UK Government now issues bonds with such clauses and is encouraging other developed and developing countries to do the same.

179. Third, these actions need to be underpinned by strong social policies: providing affordable safety nets, and action to ensure that the wishes and needs of the poor are fully considered. And this can contribute to increased social and economic stability, provide a better foundation for coping with shocks and help build the political consensus required to undertake adjustment and restore private sector confidence.

180. Fourth, following the recommendations of reports from the Financial Stability Forum (FSF) progress has been made towards better disclosure and transparency of cross-border financial flows, of the activities of highly leveraged institutions and offshore financial centres[11] (see box 8). Dealing with this will require reforms to the regulation of institutions that provide credit to highly leveraged institutions as well as raising the standards of financial supervision in offshore centres.

181. The Government welcomes the involvement of a number of developing countries in the work of the FSF, including through participation in the Forum's

---

[10] If a government defaults on its bond interest payments each individual investor has an incentive to negotiate its own repayment. This can exacerbate the crisis and leave bondholders collectively worse off. Collective action bond clauses help to avoid this by preventing a minority of bondholders blocking re-negotiation of the bond repayments in the event of default.

[11] Highly Leveraged Institutions (HLIs) borrow substantial amounts of funds relative to their asset base to invest in financial markets. They are frequently based off-shore and are subject to relatively little regulation. By investing sizeable volumes of funds they can have a significant impact in small less developed capital markets in small and medium sized economies.

BOX 8

IMPROVING GLOBAL FINANCIAL STABILITY

The Financial Stability Forum (FSF), established in 1999, brings together the finance ministries, financial regulators and central banks of major international financial centres – including the UK – to exchange information on financial market surveillance, and to address issues in financial regulation where global co-operation is important.

The UK is also a member of other international regulatory groupings such as the Basel Committee on Banking Supervision, whose Core Principles for Effective Banking Supervision represents a global standard for oversight of prudential regulation and supervision.

The Basel Committee is now reviewing its 1998 Capital Accord which underpins supervision of internationally active banks. The Accord sets out rules for the maximum levels of credit that these banks can extend. The rules take account of the type and maturity of the credit and the nature of the borrowers. An intention of the review is to align the relative treatment of credit more closely with the actual risks, including those associated with longer-term lending to developing countries.

working group on managing and monitoring capital flows. The FSF should continue to involve non-member countries in working group activities which relate to them and through consultation exercises where developing countries have particular views on a piece of Forum work.

International co-operation on investment, competition and tax

182. Progress on poverty reduction requires greater levels of international co-operation on investment, competition and tax. Almost all developing countries have embarked on unilateral liberalisation of their investment regimes with a view to attracting higher levels of investment. International agreements such as bilateral investment treaties, regional trade agreements and certain WTO provisions, such as Trade Related Investment Measures, offer the potential for increasing investor confidence in developing countries by 'locking in' policy commitments to which most countries are already committed.

183. The first comprehensive attempt to take this forward in a multilateral context was the proposed OECD Multilateral Agreement on Investment (MAI). The negotiations aimed to agree a set of principles based on non-discrimination between foreign and domestic investors, open investment regimes, investor protection and corporate behaviour.

184. There was a strong NGO campaign against the agreement. But the negotiations ultimately failed largely as a result of unresolved differences over questions of language and cultural industries. The OECD was not the appropriate forum in which to negotiate a genuinely multilateral agreement. But an international investment agreement could bring major benefits to developing countries.

185. Developing countries are already party to large numbers of bilateral investment agreements (increasingly with other developing countries), and the investor confidence that flows from these agreements brings great benefits (see figure 4.2). The UK Government believes there would be further benefits for developing countries from a multilateral investment agreement negotiated through the WTO, which works by consensus and where developing countries constitute two-thirds of the membership.

186. Such an agreement would need to be balanced and flexible. It would need to allow foreign investors the right to invest in agreed defined sectors, but recognise the rights of governments to set their own health, social and environmental standards. It would need to reflect the core principles necessary to attract sustainable investment. These are: transparency; non-discrimination (so that all who meet domestic standards can enter and operate

in the market); a degree of investor protection (for instance against the expropriation of assets without compensation); and the extent to which investment incentives and performance requirements can be used.

187. A multilateral investment agreement should not prevent governments from legislating in favour of certain regions, or targeting support for specific sectors or enterprises, where such support is available to both domestic and foreign investors. Nor should it rule out the maintenance of restrictions on foreign investment in sensitive sectors. The Government believes that an agreement along these lines is both possible and desirable.

188. The Government also believes that an international investment agreement needs to be complemented by greater international co-operation on competition policy. In a global economy, where single companies may have a very large market share in certain sectors, there is a clear need for more effective international arrangements to deal with monopoly power.

189. The UK Government and EU partners are committed to looking at these issues within the WTO and reaching an agreement on international competition policy. The core element of such an

FIGURE 4.2

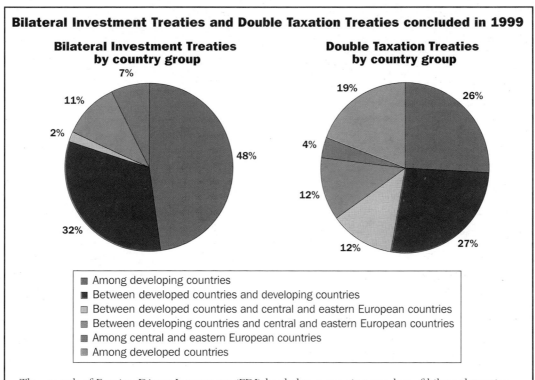

Bilateral Investment Treaties and Double Taxation Treaties concluded in 1999

Bilateral Investment Treaties by country group

7%
11%
2%
48%
32%

Double Taxation Treaties by country group

19%
26%
4%
12%
12%
27%

■ Among developing countries
■ Between developed countries and developing countries
■ Between developed countries and central and eastern European countries
■ Between developing countries and central and eastern European countries
■ Among central and eastern European countries
■ Among developed countries

The growth of Foreign Direct Investment (FDI) has led to a growing number of bilateral treaties on investment and double taxation. Many of these are between developing countries - reflecting the growth of FDI between these countries. In 1999, 96 countries signed a total of 130 Bilateral Investment Treaties, nearly half of which were between developing countries; 85 countries signed a total of 109 Double Taxation Treaties, a quarter of which were between developing countries.

Source: UNCTAD World Investment Report 2000.

agreement would be a requirement on all countries to introduce competition law.

190. As with investment, the law would need to be based on the principles of non-discrimination, national treatment and transparency. The agreement should also reflect the needs of countries at different stages of development, consensus on handling issues such as cartels and abuse of market dominance, a commitment to

co-operate across competition authorities (through the sharing of information) and increased technical assistance.

191. Taxation of the profits of transnational corporations operating in developing countries provides an important mechanism for sharing the gains from globalisation between rich and poor countries, and for reducing poverty through generating adequate revenue for investment in health and education. In the environment of highly mobile capital seeking maximum after-tax returns, developing countries are designing ever more generous and complex tax regimes to attract potential investors. There is a need for greater international co-operation to avoid this 'race to the bottom'.

192. In recent years there has been increased international co-operation in the form of bilateral taxation treaties (see figure 4.2). These protect against double tax burdens, provide certainty of treatment for cross border economic activity, and help to counter tax avoidance and evasion.

193. The conclusion of tax treaties by a developing country represents a binding commitment to international norms for taxation of income and capital. This can bring benefits in terms of increased trade and investment, as well as transfers of technology and people. The UK has 102 bilateral tax treaties – the world's largest network – of which 69 are with developing and transition economies. The UK is committed to extending coverage to include a greater number of low income countries – in particular those in Africa.

194. The Government is also seeking to promote international co-operation in information exchange about taxable income. Some countries use tax and non-

tax incentives to attract investment into the financial services sector. Often these incentives take the form of zero or only nominal taxes, together with arrangements which allow non-residents to escape tax in their country of residence. Some countries also allow the ownership of financial and corporate assets to be kept offshore.

195. These practices can offer cover for tax evasion, capital flight and the laundering of illegally acquired funds that can be particularly harmful to developing countries – depriving them of tax revenues that could be used to fund public services. A recent report by Oxfam estimated that jurisdictions operating such practices have contributed to revenue losses for developing countries of at least US$50 billion[xxii].

196. The dangers are much reduced if the financial regulators and tax authorities of all countries are committed to transparency and to the exchange of information pertinent to tax liabilities arising in other jurisdictions. From April 2001 the UK will have new powers to exchange information with the home tax authorities of non-residents. The government endorses the call by Commonwealth Finance Ministers in Malta in September 2000 for greater regional and multilateral co-operation on these issues. We will work with both the

Commonwealth Secretariat and the Commonwealth Association of Tax Administrators to this end.

Promoting corporate social responsibility

197.   The private sector has a key role in making globalisation work better for poor people.   In recent years, there has been growing public interest in corporate social responsibility. This has brought issues such as child labour, corruption, human rights, labour standards, environment and conflict into trade, investment and supply chain relationships.

198.   By applying best practice in these areas, business can play an increased role in poverty reduction and sustainable development. Many companies have also realised important commercial benefits, in terms of reputation, risk management and enhanced productivity. Greater business engagement can be encouraged by improving understanding and raising awareness of the potential benefits for business from socially responsible behaviour.

199.   Voluntary initiatives, including codes of conduct, labelling and reporting on social, environmental and economic impacts (triple bottom line reporting) are frequently undertaken with trade union, NGO and government involvement. A

number of these initiatives have created important trade opportunities, but others have acted as de facto trade barriers. A number of these difficulties have been due to insufficient understanding of the implications for developing country producers in terms of competition and compliance with these standards.

200.   Appropriate consultation and assistance programmes can maximise the opportunities for developing country producers. The UK Government, for example, provides support to programmes such as the Ethical Trading Initiative, which helps to improve working conditions in the international supply chains of its members. The Fairtrade movement has also been successful in niche markets such as coffee and chocolate.

201.   The UK Government strongly supports the revised OECD Guidelines for Multinational Enterprises. These provide norms for companies investing abroad, including compliance with the policies and laws of host countries, information disclosure, and respect for environmental sustainability, human rights and internationally recognised core labour standards. As discussed in Chapter 2 we will legislate to give UK courts jurisdiction over UK nationals who commit offences of corruption abroad. We also support the work of the United Nations Global Compact, which has developed key principles for the conduct of multinational enterprises.

202. We have introduced an amendment to UK legislation which requires pension funds to state the extent to which social, environmental or ethical considerations are taken into account in the selection, retention and realisation of investments. This should enable people saving for their own retirement to make a real contribution to responsible and sustainable global development.

203. The UK Government also encourages major companies to publish information on their environmental, social and ethical policies – something many of the largest UK firms are now doing. We strongly support this process and will establish a joint working group with both the Confederation of British Industry (CBI) and the National Association of Pension Funds, to develop guidelines for the coverage of these policy statements and their content. We will also consider whether further changes are needed in the context of the ongoing review of UK company law[xxiii, xxiv].

204. The challenge is to extend responsible business practice throughout the business community and to improve the quality and co-ordination of voluntary initiatives. The UK Government has recently appointed a Minister for Corporate Social Responsibility to promote the commercial case for greater engagement of business in this area and to co-ordinate work across the UK Government. We will be working with business to produce an integrated strategy which will consider where voluntary initiatives by business can add most value, and what should be done to promote best practice in global supply chains and in the operations of business in developing countries.

205. The UK Government has agreed to evaluate the extent to which public procurement is a cost-effective means of influencing social, health, environmental and developmental outcomes. We will also consider how far we should press for this in the EU and wider international discussions on procurement regulations and practice[xxv].

206. The UK Government has concluded a major review of the operations of the Export Credits Guarantee Department (ECGD). We will now put in place a new code of business principles in relation to ECGD covering developing countries, sustainable development, transparency, human rights, and business integrity. We are encouraging other export credit agencies within the OECD to do the same. In relation to this we are strongly supportive of the initiative in the OECD export credit group to develop guidelines for export credit agencies on the environmental and social impact of projects.

207. ECGD will report annually against its new code and will appoint a more broadly based Advisory Council to advise, develop and review ECGD's performance against the new business principles. ECGD also seeks specific undertakings from those applying or benefiting from ECGD support that bribes are not being paid, and have not been paid on the contract in question.

208. Since September 1997 the UK has ensured that official UK export credits for HIPC countries are for productive purposes only, and do not contribute to another build-up of unsustainable debt[12]. Since January 2000 this policy has been extended to other poor countries[13]. And in July 2000, at their summit in Japan, G7 leaders supported a multilateral approach to ensure that export credits to HIPCs and other low income countries are not used for unproductive purposes. This is being taken forward in the OECD, where the UK is pushing for early and substantial progress.

Encouraging private investment into developing countries

209. Even with good policies in place, it can be difficult for some developing countries to stimulate domestic investment and attract foreign investment. Foreign investors, in particular, often have exaggerated fears about the risks of investing in developing countries. Specific policies are needed to help investors to distinguish better between high and low risk environments.

210. Since 1948 the Commonwealth Development Corporation (CDC) has been the UK Government's main instrument for investing directly in commercial activities in poorer countries. In the 1997 White Paper we indicated our commitment to enlarge the resources at CDC's disposal by introducing private sector capital and turning CDC into a partnership between Government and the private sector, to encourage greater flows of beneficial investment into poorer countries.

211. The purpose of this partnership is to maximise the creation and long-term growth of viable business in developing countries (especially the poorer countries), to achieve attractive returns for shareholders in order to demonstrate that there are profitable investment opportunities in developing countries, and to implement social, environmental and ethical best practice.

212. Following the passage of the CDC Act 1999, CDC has been transformed into a public limited company. CDC is implementing a new code of business

---

[12] *Expenditure for productive purposes is defined as expenditure which contributes to a country's economic and social development.*

[13] *Poor countries refers to those eligible to borrow from the World Bank on highly concessional (IDA) terms.*

principles. CDC has also adopted a new investment policy. This requires 70 per cent of all investments to be in poor countries, and aims to make at least 50 per cent of investments in sub-Saharan Africa and south Asia. This is protected by the Government's golden share. We will continue to urge the private sector arms of the Multilateral Development Banks, such as the International Financial Corporation, to commit a higher percentage of their portfolio to the poorest countries.

213. At the same time, CDC is shifting its portfolio towards the provision of equity in private business, and is positioning itself to attract private sector involvement. The Government will invite the private sector to take a majority share-holding in CDC while retaining a substantial minority holding.

214. Trade Partners UK is encouraging British business to invest more in developing countries, and to operate in a socially and environmentally responsible

BOX 9

FINANCIAL INSTRUMENTS SUPPORTING INVESTMENT IN DEVELOPING COUNTRIES

The UK will launch an Africa Private Infrastructure Financing Facility (APIFF) in 2001. This will address the near absence of long-term lending to private infrastructure projects in sub-Saharan Africa. Unfavourable perceptions of country risk and structural obstacles within domestic financial systems can leave potentially productive investments unfunded. APIFF will operate as a senior debt fund using grant money to leverage loans from participating banks and open to other development agencies. Once a successful track record of deals has been established, we expect commercial banks to increase their lending.

The Financial Deepening Challenge Fund aims to mobilise the international and domestic financial services sector to invest in financial services in poorer countries and to make these services more accessible to the poor. The Fund is initially focused on Eastern, Central and Southern Africa and on south Asia.

The Business Linkages Challenge Fund, to be launched in early 2001, will support enterprises in developing countries to form linkages with domestic and international partners. It will facilitate knowledge transfer and improve access to the information and markets necessary to compete in a global economy.

way, and thereby to contribute to the Government's objectives for poverty reduction[14].

215. In line with this, Trade Partners UK will encourage British business to take advantage of the financial and investment mechanisms available through CDC, ECGD and the Challenge Funds discussed in box 9. A lot of progress has already been made through schemes such as the South Africa Partnership Programme. This helps small and medium sized companies from both countries to develop long-term business partnerships. We will also encourage British companies to access investment guarantees such as those available through the Multilateral Investment Guarantees Agency (MIGA) and the UK's ECGD.

---

[14] *Trade Partners UK is the trade development and investment arm of British Trade International. It has responsibility for the delivery of export support in the English regions and works closely with the devolved export support promotion organisations of Scotland, Wales and Northern Ireland.*

THE UK GOVERNMENT WILL:

- Support a country-specific approach to capital account liberalisation, that takes proper account of a country's ability to sequence and manage the risks associated with greater openness, including through helping to develop 'road maps' to guide the process.

- Support a continued IMF role in both low and middle income countries, and ensure that IMF policies support poverty reduction and sustainable development.

- Establish a new technical assistance facility, to help developing countries implement the new financial codes and standards.

- Support the inclusion of agreements on investment and competition as part of future multilateral trade negotiations in the WTO, and work in parallel to help developing countries to build capacity and encourage closer regional co-operation on these issues.

- Work to build support for consultations beyond the OECD with developing countries on taxation issues, and extend the coverage of the UK's bilateral tax treaties to include more low countries.

- Continue to strengthen our work to promote corporate social responsibility, particularly with regard to greater disclosure of social, environmental and ethical policies.

- Establish the Commonwealth Development Corporation as a vibrant public/private partnership providing equity financing in the poorest countries, and develop a new facility to improve the availability of long-term debt finance for private sector investment in infrastructure in Africa.

CAPTURING GAINS FROM TRADE

> *The UK Government will:*
>
> - **Support an open and rules-based international trading system, and work to promote equitable trade rules and an effective voice for developing countries.**
>
> - **Support continuing reductions in barriers to trade, both in developed and developing countries, and work to improve the capacity of developing countries to take advantage of new trade opportunities.**

Using trade to reduce poverty

216. A key element of globalisation has been the reduction in barriers to trade. Over the last 50 years, tariff and non-tariff barriers have been reduced substantially, including through a series of multilateral trade rounds. Although significant restrictions remain, these reductions have created real development opportunities. Trade has a vital role to play in helping developing countries to boost their economic growth and to generate the resources necessary for reducing poverty.

217. In the 1950s and 1960s, protectionist policies in developing countries – promoting industrialisation by restricting imports of manufactures – were often associated with quite rapid growth. But the gains were unequally distributed, with the poor often being hurt by the discrimination against agriculture. And these policies eventually hit limits of market size and loss of contact with advances in world technology.

218. This is one of the reasons why, in the last few decades, there has been a marked trend towards greater trade openness. And this has been associated with faster economic growth in the countries concerned (see figure 5.1). For this White Paper, the UK Government commissioned a review of recent research evidence on the effects of trade and trade policy on poverty[xxvi]. The broad conclusions of this review can be summarised in the following points:

- on average, the poor benefit from increased trade openness in the same proportion as richer households. But, because this is an average, there are cases where poor people gain from trade less than proportionately and cases in which they gain more than proportionately. For policy-makers the key challenge is to reduce the former and increase the latter.

- reduction of a country's own trade barriers tends to bring real benefits to its consumers, including poor consumers.

- while the effects of trade reform tend to be positive, especially in the medium and long term, it can have significant adverse effects on particular groups, especially in the short term.

CAPTURING GAINS FROM TRADE

FIGURE 5.1

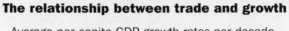

The relationship between trade and growth

Average per capita GDP growth rates per decade.

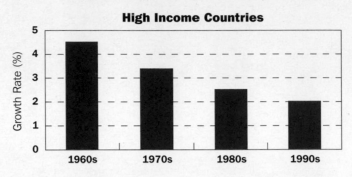

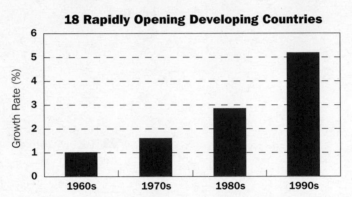

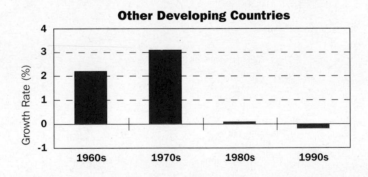

In a group of 18 developing countries that became much more open to trade after 1980, as measured by rising shares of exports and imports in GDP, the average growth rate accelerated. This group includes most of the world's poor people - among the 18 countries are Bangladesh, China, India, Ghana, Nepal, Uganda, and Vietnam - and since 1990, this group has been catching up with rich countries, whose growth has slowed.

By contrast, other developing countries on average became only slightly more open to trade after 1980, and their growth dropped to near zero, so that they fell further behind the rich countries. A wide range of policies and circumstances contributed to the better performance of the 18 countries, but the association between their increased openness and their faster growth is striking, and is confirmed by more detailed statistical analysis.

Source: Dollar & Kraay (forthcoming), Trade, Growth & Poverty

- these potential adverse effects will inform the process of trade opening – in terms of sequencing, speed and accompanying policies. They should certainly encourage governments to invest in education and skills to equip people to take advantage of new employment opportunities, and to provide adequate safety nets to protect the poor during the process of change.
- trade openness, especially import liberalisation, generally has beneficial effects on productivity, the adoption and use of technology, and investment – and this is an important channel through which trade openness stimulates economic growth.
- the extent to which trade openness contributes to poverty reduction depends on broader economic and social circumstances and policies. So trade openness is a necessary but not sufficient condition for poverty reduction. And trade policy needs to be situated within the wider development context.

Realising export potential

219. The fastest growing developing countries in recent decades have been those which promoted exports. It is in these countries – mainly east Asian – that poverty has fallen most rapidly.

220. There is still great scope for expansion of trade by poor countries. In 1998, the total exports of south Asia's 1.3 billion people were roughly equal to those of Thailand's 60 million people, and the total exports of sub-Saharan Africa's 600 million were scarcely more than those of Malaysia's 20 million.

221. Not all developing countries will go down the same path as east Asia, which has a comparative advantage in manufactured exports because it is densely populated. With little land per person, there is less scope for primary exports than for labour-intensive production of industrial exports. South Asia too is densely populated and has good prospects for growth of manufactured exports, which could create many millions of jobs for people with just a basic education[xxvii]. The same could apply to some densely populated countries in Africa.

222. But for countries where land is abundant relative to labour, including most of those in Africa and Latin America, the best export prospects over the next few decades are in natural-resource-based products. World demand for primary products will grow, partly because of rapid economic growth in land-scarce Asia. For developing countries to gain from this, however, developed countries must end the large subsidies to their farmers, which currently distort world prices and deter private investment in agriculture in poor countries. In some primary sectors, moreover, processing is discouraged by higher tariffs on processed products in developed countries. These should be reduced.

223. To increase their primary exports, developing countries also need help to modernise their agriculture and make it more competitive. For instance, research enabled Malaysia to do well in commodities such as palm oil and cocoa, in which Africa fell behind technically. Primary-exporting countries need help, too, to design effective ways of managing the risks of fluctuations in world commodity prices, since attempts to stabilise prices at the international level have proved unsustainable.

224. Diversification of primary exports can also reduce risk. Non-traditional agricultural items such as out of season fruits and vegetables are particularly promising: demand in developed countries is growing fast and imports are less restricted. Growing them – on their land or as workers on large farms – generates new income opportunities for poor people in rural areas. Washing, cutting, packaging and labelling can add value and provide more jobs. To diversify their primary exports, however, countries again need access to technical expertise, as well as good transport links.

225. Costa Rica is an example of a country that successfully diversified its primary exports. Initially heavily reliant on a few staples such as bananas, coffee and beef, it now sells a remarkable range of non-traditional agricultural items to the US market. This was helped by universal basic education, which made Costa Rica's farmers and workers more adaptable, as well as by specialised research and training in relevant sectors[xxviii]. Educating its people

BOX 10

GLOBALISATION, JOBS, AND WOMEN

The expansion of world trade has brought employment dividends for women. Women's employment has grown at a faster pace than men's in the last 20 years. In 1978, for example, Bangladesh had only four garment factories. By 1995, it had 2,400, employing 1.2 million workers, 90 per cent of them women.

These are significant gains for women, but many challenges remain. Studies of women garment workers in south Asia show that almost half of them hand over their wages to their husband, or another male member of the household. And many women have to cope with a 'double day', combining paid work with an undiminished burden of household work and child care. Furthermore, women's wages are consistently lower than men's.

Poor information flows, combined with low levels of literacy and limited skills development and training, act as barriers to women's economic advancement. Without more investment in female education, women could become locked into low-skilled, low paid, and insecure work. But with more investment, and with access to credit and other assets, women can gain real advantages from the opening up of world trade.

also enabled Costa Rica to diversify into exports of manufacturers and services, a long-term strategy which could and should be pursued by other primary-export countries.

Creating a fairer international trading system and reforming the WTO

226. Support for open trade is not to be confused with unregulated trade. On the contrary, if open trade is to work for the world's poor we need effective multilateral trade rules made by an institution in which developing countries are properly represented, and an institution capable of enforcing them, for poor countries and rich countries alike. This is precisely what the World Trade Organisation (WTO) is and represents. The WTO is a membership-based organisation which takes decisions on the basis of consensus. Developing countries are a majority of its 140 members. A further 30 developing and transition countries have applied to join.

227. It is true that the WTO still bears the heavy imprint of the much smaller group of mainly northern countries that have dominated negotiations since the founding of the General Agreement on Tariffs and Trade (GATT). And it is true that the WTO should be more transparent and open and its rules easier to understand.

228. But it is essential that we retain, strengthen and reform the WTO and the

rules-based system, and ensure that it works for poor countries. The alternative is a situation in which the rich and powerful dominate the rest, or where the richer economies make bilateral trade deals between themselves and exclude the poorest.

229. We will also urge the WTO to commit itself, with the rest of the international community, to achieving the International Development Targets. This would send a powerful signal of its commitment to poverty reduction and acknowledge that trade is a means to an end, not an end in itself.

230. There are substantial inequities in the existing international trading system. Developed countries have long preached the virtues of openness: but practice lags behind the rhetoric. Despite progress over the last 50 years, developed countries maintain significant tariff and non-tariff barriers against the exports of developing countries.

231. These barriers are most damaging in areas of key importance to developing countries, such as agriculture, textiles and clothing, while the use and threat of 'trade defence' instruments (e.g. anti-dumping) creates further obstacles[15]. Total developing country gains from a 50 per cent cut in tariffs, by both developed and developing countries, would be in the order of $150 billion – around three times aid flows[xxix].

---

[15] *A product is considered to have been 'dumped' if the export price is less than the price charged in the producing country for the same product. The WTO rules allow countries to levy extra duties on imported goods if they can establish that they are being dumped and if the imports are causing 'material injury' to domestic industry.*

CAPTURING GAINS FROM TRADE

The use of subsidies, especially in the agriculture and fisheries sectors, often encourages unsustainable production in developed countries too.

232. While the failure of the WTO Ministerial Conference at Seattle in 1999 was a serious setback – from which lessons should be learned – it would be a great mistake if the world community were to give up on a future multilateral trade round. The world's poorest countries have much to gain from a broad-based multilateral trade round, and would be badly hit by a retreat into trade protectionism.

233. Two lessons in particular stand out from Seattle. First, developed countries must give greater weight to the needs of developing countries whose agreement will be needed if another Round is to be launched. Second, developing countries, who now make up a majority of WTO members, could make significant gains from a new Round if they can exert their influence more effectively.

234. The UK will continue to press for a pro-development EU negotiating position in a new Trade Round, which includes substantial cuts in high tariffs and in trade-distorting subsidies, particularly for those sectors of most importance to developing countries. This could make it genuinely a 'Development Round'.

235. This means giving high priority to the multilateral liberalisation of agriculture, addressing both quotas and tariffs, and opening service sectors to competition. Both of these areas are part of the built-in agenda under the Uruguay Round. We also think that a new Round should be broad enough to handle other issues where there are important potential benefits to developing countries, including industrial tariffs – particularly textiles and clothing, rules on anti-dumping, government procurement and trade facilitation (streamlining of customs procedures). For reasons explained in Chapter 4, we think it should include investment and competition too. It should also clarify the relationship between trade and multilateral environment agreements.

236. The WTO can help poor countries to challenge discriminatory practices on the part of stronger trading partners. While there is room for improvement, there is now a functioning system for settling disputes between countries, which developing countries can and do use. The UK Government was instrumental in getting international agreement to the establishment of an Advisory Centre on WTO Law. This will help poor countries to bring cases under the Dispute Settlement Procedures of the WTO, and to exercise their rights, on more equal terms, within the rules-based system.

237. Some developing countries face genuine difficulties in implementing commitments made under the Uruguay Round Agreement. Where developing countries are committed to implementation but face these difficulties, we will support flexibility on deadlines and well-targeted technical assistance to assist with necessary reforms. We also support detailed discussions on possible changes to agreements to accommodate developing country concerns, as currently being taken forward under the WTO Implementation Review Mechanism.

238. In a new Round, the UK and our EU partners will support an approach that recognises more explicitly that WTO members are at different stages of development. To help countries manage their commitments we will press for special and differential provisions to be real and binding, and for any new WTO rules to reflect countries' implementation capacity. In the longer term, the WTO needs to consider a more workable set of country categories to take better into account different levels of development.

239. To create a fairer multilateral trading system, an urgent priority must be to strengthen the capacity of developing countries to participate effectively in the WTO and the international trading system. 23 least-developed country members of the WTO have no representation in Geneva, where there can be more than 40 meetings a week across a diverse range of subjects.

240. We will work with developing countries and other development agencies to help build trade policy capacity in both national capitals and in Geneva. This is essential if poorer countries are to protect and promote their interests more effectively in a new Trade Round. The UK Government will double its support in this area from £15 million over the last three years, to £30 million over the next three years. As part of this increased effort, we will launch in early 2001 a new Africa Trade and Poverty Programme. This will provide technical support for national governments and regional organisations in sub-Saharan Africa in order to help build capacity for the formulation of trade policy and for international trade negotiation.

Promoting a pro-development EU policy on trade

241. The European Commission negotiates on behalf of all EU members, including the UK, in multilateral and bilateral trade negotiations. This includes developing and managing preferential trade regimes such as the Cotonou Agreement with African, Caribbean and Pacific (ACP) countries or the Generalised System of Preferences (GSP), as well as bilateral free trade agreements between countries or groups of countries. The Commission also manages the Common Agricultural Policy (CAP) and many product standards are set at the European level. Getting a pro-development EU position across this wide range of trade issues is of enormous importance in securing a fairer deal for poor countries from international trade and in a future multilateral Trade Round.

242. The EU has over 30 different trade regimes. The aims vary: for the GSP and the Cotonou Agreement the drive is primarily developmental, whereas other agreements have a domestic economic and political motivation. The Government continues to push for the EU's bilateral free trade agreements to be consistent with our wider development goals.

243. The GSP was set up to give developing countries additional tariff preferences on their exports into the EU. However, many products are excluded from the scheme, and it is difficult and complex to use. We will press for removal or further reduction of tariffs, a simplification of product categories, the elimination of sector graduation, and less onerous regulations on rules of origin for imports. In consultation with business and developing country partners, we will work to make the scheme more accessible and user-friendly to exporters and importers.

244. Recently the Commission put forward a proposal to allow all exports from least developed countries (LDCs) into the EU duty free, except arms. This is an important initiative and should help build confidence in a New Trade Round and also to increase economic activity in LDCs. The UK has consistently supported duty-free access for LDCs, and is pressing for EU agreement for the Commission's proposal

as soon as possible. We recognise that this will create adjustment challenges for some of the non-least developed countries in the ACP group, and we will work to ensure provision of sustainable assistance to help them in the adjustment process.

245. The EU's Common Agricultural Policy is a barrier to the access of developing countries to our markets. The United Nations Conference on Trade and Development (UNCTAD) has estimated that the agricultural policies of OECD countries – even after the Uruguay Round reforms – cost developing countries $20 billion per year. Similarly, while imports of raw fish from developing countries face low tariffs, tariffs rise substantially for processed fish and non-tariff barriers are also significant. The Common Fisheries Policy (CFP) subsidises the EU fishing industry, making it difficult for developing countries to compete, and contributing to over-fishing. We will use every opportunity to work for change to the CAP and CFP.

246. The Commission also investigates complaints of unfair dumping and subsidies under EC Regulations, which are in turn based on WTO rules. Developing countries are concerned that anti-dumping and anti-subsidy measures are supplanting tariffs as a new form of protectionism. The UK Government believes that anti-dumping and anti-subsidy cases should be considered on the basis of the economic evidence. We will oppose any attempt to use these measures as a form of covert protectionism. We will also maintain our position that quota protection for textiles and clothing, which must be eliminated by the agreed deadline of 2005, should not be replaced by new forms of protection.

Helping poor people to trade

247. Reducing policy barriers – in developing countries themselves, as well as in developed countries – is important, but not enough to guarantee expansion of trade. For example, under the Lomé Convention the EU gave preferential market access to African, Caribbean and Pacific countries, but exports from these countries to the EU fell from £16 billion in 1985 to £14 billion in 1994[xxx]. We therefore also need to help remove other barriers that prevent poor people from engaging in trade, or from increasing production in response to new market opportunities.

248. Transport costs are often a particular obstacle to trade. For instance, Uganda's distance from the sea and its inadequate rail and road connections impose the equivalent of a tax of 80 per cent on exports of clothing, textiles and footwear to world markets[xxxi]. In Indian ports, average ship turn-around time in 1993 was four to ten days, compared with six to eight hours in Singapore. On average across countries, a halving of transport costs is estimated almost to double the volume of trade[xxxii].

249. Within countries, too, high transport costs exclude poor people from trade. For example, many villages in central

FIGURE 5.2

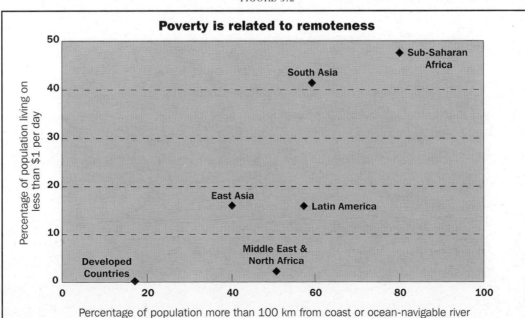

Source: Geographical data: Gallup and Sachs 1998 'Geography and Economic Development' for all except MENA and Developed Countries (calculated from Gallup and Sachs data). Poverty data: World Bank, WDI 2000 (figure for Developed Countries assumed to be zero). Developed countries are Western Europe plus US, Canada, Japan, Australia and New Zealand.

India still lack all-weather roads, which prevents them from trading regularly with other nearby villages and towns, let alone with other countries. And across the world, poverty rates tend to be higher in more remote regions (figure 5.2). Better transport and communications links within countries, as well as between them, are essential to spread the gains from increases in trade – with improvements in rural roads a particular priority.

250. To lower transport costs requires investment in ports and airports, roads and railways. In many developing countries, it also requires improved maintenance and management of existing transport infrastructure. In both respects, greater involvement of the private sector, in partnership with governments, is crucial.

251. The same point applies to other infrastructure which developing countries will need to improve if they are to reap the benefits of globalisation, such as water, energy supply and telecommunications. A particular problem for the private sector is raising the long-term loans needed to invest in infrastructure projects. In response to this, the UK Government has been instrumental in the formation of the multi-donor funded Public-Private Infrastructure Advisory Facility to help developing countries to improve the environment for private investment in infrastructure. (See also Box 10 in

Chapter 4 on the Africa Private Infrastructure Financing Facility).

Making trade and non-trade standards serve development

252. It is reasonable that consumers are pressing for more information on products and tighter safety and hygiene standards. And it is right that consumers should be concerned about the processes by which products are made – in terms of both labour standards and the environment. It is this interest which has led to the rapid growth of the ethical trading and consumer movements, particularly in developed countries.

253. However, developing country exporters find the proliferation of regulations and standards hard to comply with. And they fear that 'process standards' on the way products are made (such as on labour, the environment or animal welfare) will lock their products out of developed country markets. A balance needs to be struck which provides adequate information and quality to consumers but which enables developing countries to export and grow their way out of poverty.

254. The UK Government is committed to the promotion of core labour standards worldwide, and we strongly endorse the efforts of the ILO to extend the enforcement of core labour standards in all countries (see Chapter 2). But imposing trade sanctions on poor countries that do not fully comply with all labour standards would punish countries for their poverty, and hurt the poorest most.

255. The Government is committed to promoting social, health and environmental standards and to maintaining a fair and open multilateral trading system. We also take seriously developing countries' concerns about the potential for the misuse of environmental measures for protectionist purposes. We believe that trade agreements and multilateral environment agreements should be mutually supportive and have equal status. Through multilateral negotiations, we will press for clarification of the relationship between WTO and multilateral environmental agreement rules. We will also press for clarification in the WTO of how trade rules affect product labelling, including eco-labelling.

256. We are working through the EU and the WTO to reduce all forms of trade-distorting subsidies, and will consider what further action may be needed in order to phase out environmentally damaging subsidies in particular. We support the undertaking of sustainability impact assessments of trade policy changes and will help developing countries to integrate environmental management into their export strategies.

THE UK GOVERNMENT WILL:

- Urge the WTO to commit itself with the rest of the international community to achieving the International Development Targets.

- Work to make the next multilateral Trade Round a 'Development Round' – that brings real development benefits to developing countries, across a wide range of issues.

- Work in the WTO and other international bodies to identify and remove subsidies which harm poor producers and provide perverse economic incentives resulting in the unsustainable use of natural resources.

- Work to improve the access of developing countries to EU markets, including duty and quota-free access to EU markets for all least developed countries, the removal of quotas on textiles and clothing by the agreed deadline of 2005, tighter application of the rules controlling anti-dumping measures, and continuing liberalisation of preferential trade arrangements.

- Push for significant reform of the CAP, leading to the reduction as soon as possible of domestic and export subsidies on EU agricultural products, as well as tariff and non-tariff barriers to imports from developing countries.

- Work within the WTO to ensure much greater account is taken of developing country circumstances in rule-making.

- Press for trade policy – and complementary economic, social and political policies – to be built into developing countries' poverty reduction strategies.

- Work with others to strengthen the capacity of developing countries to participate in international negotiations and to take advantage of new trading opportunities, including through improved infrastructure and transport links.

- Maintain our opposition to the use of trade sanctions to enforce core labour standards, and oppose any protectionist misuse of environmental standards.

TACKLING GLOBAL ENVIRONMENTAL PROBLEMS

The UK Government will:

- **Work to reduce the contribution made by developed countries to global environmental degradation.**

- **Work with developing countries to ensure that their poverty reduction strategies reflect the need to manage environmental resources sustainably, and strengthen their capacity to participate in international negotiations.**

Meeting our own responsibilities

257. Globalisation is creating new challenges for the management of the global environment. Existing patterns of production and consumption are placing enormous strains on the global eco-system, and rapid population growth is adding to these pressures. Well-managed, globalisation can help to address these challenges – by promoting greater development, increasing the resources and information available for improved environmental management, and by helping to spread cleaner technology.

258. The sustainable management of the planet is a clear example of a global public good (see box 13). The survival of the species depends upon a healthy global environment. The ozone layer screens out ultraviolet rays. Eco-systems help purify air and water resources, and convert waste. And the earth's biodiversity provides a store of medicines and food products, maintaining genetic variety that reduces vulnerability to diseases. But we are degrading the global environment that provides these life-sustaining services for us.

259. Developed and developing countries have a common interest therefore in specific policies and competent institutions to help ensure that the management of globalisation is environmentally sustainable and that it does not produce irrevocable damage to fragile environmental resources. Our shared goal must be to meet the economic needs of the present without compromising the ability of the planet to provide for the needs of future generations.

260. That requires a new focus on equity. The poor contribute least to environmental problems, yet are the most vulnerable to their ill effects. They are forced to live in the most degraded and ecologically fragile areas. And they are least able to cope with harmful impacts that affect their health and livelihoods, such as water scarcity, indoor air pollution, lack of sanitation, eroded land and the loss of living species. Environmental degradation also leaves the poor more vulnerable to natural disasters. In its 1998 annual report, the Red Cross estimated that for the first time the number of refugees from natural disasters exceeded those displaced as a result of war.

261. It is the consumption patterns of people in developed countries that currently make the major contribution to global environmental degradation – although the economic growth of major developing countries is increasing their own contribution. Industrialised countries, including the UK, have a particular responsibility therefore to minimise their environmentally damaging behaviour.

FIGURE 6.1

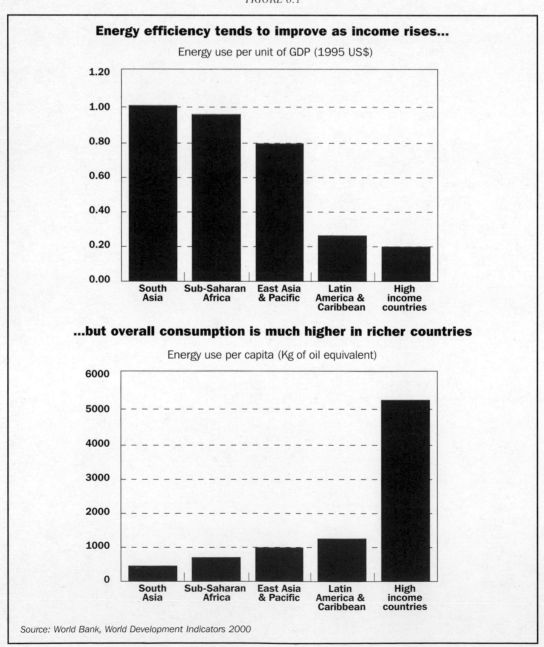

Energy efficiency tends to improve as income rises...

Energy use per unit of GDP (1995 US$)

...but overall consumption is much higher in richer countries

Energy use per capita (Kg of oil equivalent)

Source: World Bank, World Development Indicators 2000

TACKLING GLOBAL ENVIRONMENTAL PROBLEMS

262. This means reducing our contribution to harmful climate change, pollution and resource-depletion. It also means moving towards more sustainable consumption and production patterns. The Government's Strategy for Sustainable Development will help achieve these objectives. In addition the Government will review how the UK can increase its productivity in the use of natural resources, focusing in particular on renewable energy. But we and others have much more still to do[xxxiii].

263. There has been important progress in some areas, including reductions in domestic greenhouse gas emissions. We will meet our Kyoto target of a 12.5 per cent reduction in greenhouse gas emissions, and move beyond it towards our goal of reducing the UK's CO_2 emissions by 20 per cent by 2010[16]. The outcome of the UN Climate Conference in The Hague in November 2000 was disappointing, but progress was made on all issues, including those of particular relevance to developing countries. We hope that agreement will be reached when talks resume in 2001.

Integrating environmental sustainability into development planning

264. Developing countries are already experiencing problems of environmental degradation and exhaustion of environmental resources which are vital to their long-term development. As their economies grow, these problems will increase unless there is a greater focus on the sustainability of their development. Eastern Europe and central Asian countries have an enormously costly environmental legacy. Economic decline and deteriorating government capacity have meant that environmental problems in general, and industrial pollution in particular, have not been addressed.

265. Developing countries need strengthened capacity to manage their natural resources and negotiate in international forums. Chapter 7 underlines the central role of country-owned poverty reduction strategies. It is important that these strategies are sustainable and integrate environmental concerns. The World Bank needs to strengthen its capacity to take account of sustainable development in supporting poverty reduction strategies. And the IMF must be aware of these linkages in designing their programmes.

266. Development agencies should provide technical assistance to developing country governments to put in place the institutional framework necessary to promote consistent approaches to the environment across different government ministries, and to implement and enforce environmental laws and regulations. This includes helping to ensure that companies pay the true cost of their pollution to the environment.

---

[16] *Under the Kyoto Protocol, adopted in December 1997, developed countries agreed to reduce their emissions of six greenhouse gases by an average of 5.2 per cent against 1990 levels. Reductions are to be achieved by the period 2008-2012.*

267. Effective regulatory mechanisms are particularly important for those countries whose comparative advantage lies in natural resource exports, in environmentally sensitive sectors such as agriculture, minerals, forestry, fisheries and tourism.

268. Sustainable management of these resources can bring real benefits to poor people. In Ghana, for example, the UK Government is helping to promote sustainable timber production. The programme is leading to changes in forest concession rules and royalties, so that local communities get greater control over

BOX 11

GLOBALISATION AND WATER RESOURCES [17]

Freshwater is a limited and precious resource. With an increasing global population and the risks associated with climate change, the challenge of managing water resources grows. Many poor people do not have access to sufficient quantities for consumption and production. With climate change, the risks and uncertainties will be greater. Water is already a contested resource: in many regions of the world the lack of freshwater has reached crisis proportions and can be a cause of outright conflict.

World map showing countries vulnerability to water stress projected for the year 2025

Based on data produced for the UN Commission on Sustainable Development

(Raskin et al 1997) "Water Futures: Assessment of long range patterns and problems" Stockholm Environment Institute

☐ Limited or no vulnerability to water stress

■ Vulnerable to water stress

■ High vulnerability to water stress

Increased awareness of these issues has prompted a greater focus on achieving environmental and financial sustainability, more sustainable access for the poor, and better water management. The key challenge is how to mobilise governments to share and provide water whilst ensuring that its management at a local level is effective and equitable.

The UK Government supports closer regional and international co-operation, for example the Global Water Partnership which promotes the sustainable management of water through improved dialogue and knowledge dissemination.

[17] *For more detail of UK policy in this area see the DFID strategy paper on 'Addressing the Water Crisis'. www.dfid.gov.uk.*

logging on their land and a greater share of the financial benefits.

Working with the private sector

269. The role of the private sector in promoting better environmental management is vital. It has a responsibility to improve the efficiency of its resource use, to manage its environmental impacts, to promote the spread of clean technologies and to help disseminate international best practice.

270. Change has come from a business recognition that improved environmental practices can lead to lower costs and thus enhance competitiveness; and from growing consumer demand for goods and services produced in environmentally sustainable ways. This is stimulating action to improve environmental standards throughout the supply chain. Increasing numbers of companies are also incorporating a commitment to sustainable development into their business principles and activities.

271. This includes the introduction of environmental management systems, setting clear targets for reduced pollution and waste, and the publication of environmental audits, which help the public hold companies to account for their environmental performance. The most significant shift so far has come from larger companies, including the transnationals.

This in turn is having some positive knock-on effect on enterprises in developing countries. We will continue to encourage the development of sustainable and growing markets for affordable, cleaner and more resource-efficient technologies, particularly to tackle those environmental problems which most affect the poor. We will also continue to promote mechanisms which increase incentives for the private sector to be more environmentally responsible.

272. But voluntary action is not enough. Without effective regulation in developing countries, many companies, not least many national and state-owned enterprises, continue to degrade the environment. Much more needs to be done to ensure that true environmental costs are reflected in prices.

International co-operation on the environment

273. Action on global environmental problems also requires greater international co-operation. In recent years, an increasing range of international agreements has been developed, such as the conventions on climate change, biodiversity and ozone depletion.

274. But developing countries – those who suffer most from the effects of these environmental problems – need to have a more effective voice in international environmental negotiations. And they need more support in assessing the implications of environmental degradation for their people.

275. Developing country governments are increasingly concerned that industrialised countries wish to impose environmental conditions that will prevent their development. Further international agreements on the environment will become more difficult if developing countries do not believe such agreements are in their interests. The ten-year follow-up to the Conference on Environment and Development (Rio + 10) will be held in 2002. This presents a real opportunity to make further progress on integrating the environment and development agendas.

276. Developed countries have already agreed to meet emissions targets under the Kyoto Protocol, but much bigger cuts will be needed if atmospheric concentrations of greenhouse gases are to be stabilised. Many of the effects of climate change are uncertain and could vary greatly between regions. But the effects on poor countries are likely to be very damaging. Rising sea levels, changes in rainfall, loss of subsistence crops and increased disease are likely to hit poor people hardest.

277. Measures have to be taken to reduce future emissions in all countries. The private sector has a crucial role to play here. The Clean Development Mechanism of the Kyoto Protocol encourages companies to invest in emission-reducing projects in developing countries by giving the investing country credit against targets for the reductions achieved. But we must also support developing countries in assessing the likely impacts of climate change and to build capacity to minimise the threat to their territory and people.

278. We should look critically at how global institutions deal with environmental issues. There is a clear need for better co-ordination among the Multilateral

BOX 12

RENEWABLE ENERGY INITIATIVE

The G8 Renewable Energy Task Force was established at the Okinawa Summit in July 2000 to identify ways of improving the supply, distribution and use of renewable energy in developing countries. Its aims are: firstly, to tackle the lack of access to commercial energy in developing countries; and, secondly, to prevent the future air quality and climate change problems which would arise if all these new consumers were supplied with energy from fossil fuels.

The Task Force will identify barriers to the development of sustainable markets for renewable energy in developing countries, and ways of reducing or removing these obstacles. Increasing the supply of renewable energy will improve the lives of the 2 billion people who do not have access to commercial energy by reducing pollution, supporting new jobs and giving new opportunities for education – including through the use of information technology.

Environmental Agreements. Actions should be geared towards strengthening existing institutions and delivering practical solutions which address real problems on the ground. It is essential that the policies and programmes of the main multilateral agencies reflect the need to manage environmental resources sustainably.

279. A good example of international co-operation on environmental issues has been the establishment of the Global Environment Facility (GEF). This assists developing countries in meeting the additional cost to their national economy of addressing global environmental objectives. The GEF has built up substantial experience in practical approaches to global environmental problems. The UK Government is committed to providing support for the GEF to improve its performance, to ensure it is more responsive to the needs of developing countries, and to enable it to combat global environmental problems more effectively. The UK will take an active and positive part in the negotiations for the third replenishment of the GEF, which will be completed by early 2002.

THE UK GOVERNMENT WILL:

- Use Rio + 10 to endorse the International Development Targets and reinforce progress towards sustainable development.

- Deliver its Kyoto target and move beyond it towards our goal of reducing the UK's CO_2 emissions by 20 per cent by 2010.

- Work with developing countries and the IMF and World Bank to better integrate environmental sustainability into poverty reduction strategies.

- Help least developed countries to benefit from the Clean Development Mechanism, and consider further ways of improving developing countries' access to clean and sustainable energy sources in light of the report of the G8 task force on Renewable Energy.

- Work with business to increase their opportunities to be environmentally responsible.

- Increase our assistance to least developed countries to help them participate more effectively in the negotiation of multilateral environmental agreements, and benefit from their implementation.

- Press for a 50 per cent increase in resources for the third replenishment of the Global Environment Facility from 2002 to 2006.

A more detailed account of the UK's policy on environment and sustainable development is set out in the DFID strategy paper: 'Achieving sustainability: poverty elimination and the environment' and 'Addressing the Water Crisis'.

USING DEVELOPMENT ASSISTANCE MORE EFFECTIVELY

The UK Government will:

- Increase its development assistance to 0.33 per cent as a proportion of GNP by 2003/04, and continue to make progress towards the 0.7 per cent UN target.

- Work to increase the proportion of global development assistance spent in poor countries, help to improve its effectiveness and to reduce the burdens placed on recipient countries, end UK tied aid and work for multilateral untying.

- Introduce a new Development Bill to replace the outdated Overseas Development and Co-operation Act (1980), to consolidate our poverty focused approach to development.

- Provide faster and more substantial debt relief for heavily indebted poor countries that are committed to poverty reduction.

Focusing development assistance on poverty reduction

280. Globalisation has led to a huge growth in private financial flows, including to developing countries, but many of the poorest countries are failing to attract these flows.

281. Domestic savings are the main source of finance for investment throughout the developing world (see figures 7.1 and 7.2). Many middle income countries, such as those in Latin America and Eastern Europe, are better able to supplement these resources by attracting private investment and loans from developed country governments and international financial institutions. Poorer countries, such as those in south Asia and sub-Saharan Africa, not only have much lower savings but have little or no access to foreign investment and lending.

282. Development assistance is a vital resource that can help put in place the reforms necessary to attract inward investment, improve government services, boost economic growth, and equip them to take advantage of new opportunities in a global economy[18].

283. But making development assistance more effective in reducing poverty requires some important changes in its use and allocation. The global pool of development assistance has averaged $60 billion a year over the last five years. This can and must be better used.

---

[18] 'Development assistance' is used interchangeably with 'aid' to mean concessional financial flows to developing countries – termed Official Development Assistance (oda) – and countries in transition (principally certain countries in Central and Eastern Europe and the new Independent States of the former Soviet Union) – termed Official Aid (oa). Concessional flows are grants or loans with at least a 35% grant element. Developing countries which are partially creditworthy (primarily middle income countries) also have access to loans on near commercial terms (ie non-concessional flows) from developed countries and international financial institutions.

FIGURE 7.1

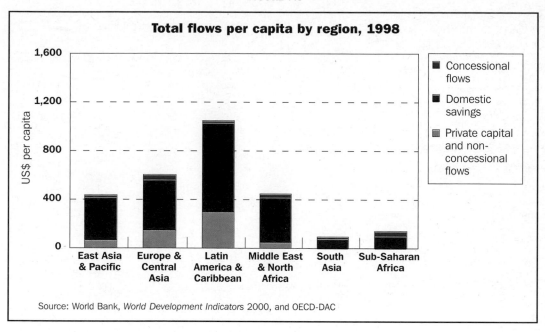

Source: World Bank, *World Development Indicators* 2000, and OECD-DAC

FIGURE 7.2

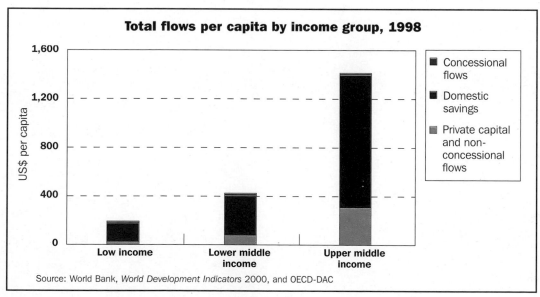

Source: World Bank, *World Development Indicators* 2000, and OECD-DAC

284. Too much global development assistance is still used to sweeten commercial contracts or to serve short-term political interests. Too much is allocated to middle income countries at the expense of the poorest. A significant proportion remains tied to the purchase of goods and services from the donor country, reducing the value and distorting the use of that aid. And too much development

BOX 13

IMPROVING THE ALLOCATION OF DEVELOPMENT ASSISTANCE

Development agencies have taken notice of the link between aid effectiveness, poverty and the policy environment. Over the last ten years there has been a striking improvement in the targeting of development assistance on poor countries with broadly acceptable policies.

But we could do better. Recent research by the World Bank suggests that a further refocusing of global development assistance on this basis could lift as many people out of poverty as could be achieved by a 50 per cent increase in present development assistance budgets[xxxiv]. Too much assistance is still allocated to relatively wealthy countries with poor policies and there remains a bias towards small countries which means that countries with very large numbers of poor people receive less assistance per capita.

For example, figure 7.3 shows that large countries in south Asia receive only $10 of development assistance per poor person per year, compared to $950 in the Middle East and North Africa. Moreover, this understates the extent of the distortion, as assistance going to the Middle East and North Africa is less well targeted on poor people.

assistance is used to fund isolated donor-led projects rather than helping governments to implement long-term programmes of poverty reduction.

285. There has been a shift in the policy of some development agencies in recent years, but there is still considerable room for improvement – in focusing more aid on the poorest, particularly on those developing countries that are pursuing good policies and where there are large numbers of poor people (see box 13). We have also learned by experience that

FIGURE 7.3

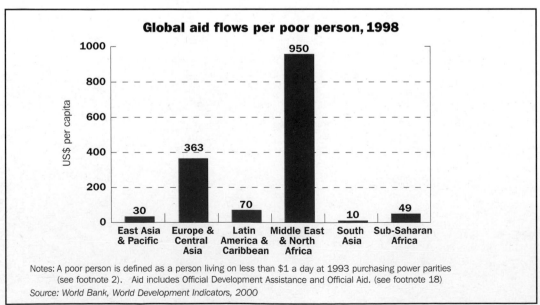

Global aid flows per poor person, 1998

Notes: A poor person is defined as a person living on less than $1 a day at 1993 purchasing power parities (see footnote 2). Aid includes Official Development Assistance and Official Aid. (see footnote 18)
Source: World Bank, World Development Indicators, 2000

USING DEVELOPMENT ASSISTANCE MORE EFFECTIVELY

development assistance works best when it supports a development strategy designed and led by the national government in consultation with its civil society[xxxv]. Both national governments and development agencies need to adjust their strategies to meet the challenges of globalisation.

286. The UK Government has already made a radical shift in its own approach to development assistance. Between 1997/98 and 2003/04, our development assistance budget will rise by 45 per cent in real terms, totalling £3.6 billion in the final year – the largest UK development assistance budget ever in real as well as cash terms. Development assistance as a proportion of GNP will rise to 0.33 per cent in 2003/04, up from 0.26 per cent in 1997. We are thus beginning to fulfil our commitment to meet the UN 0.7 per cent oda/gnp target.

287. We are also focusing these resources on systematic poverty reduction. In 1999/2000 we spent 74 per cent of the UK's development assistance in low income countries, up from 68 per cent in 1996/97[19]. We will further increase the focus on low income countries over the next three years. And we have increased our capacity to provide more resources to countries that implement pro-poor policies by establishing policy and performance funds for Africa, Asia and for the

multilateral development institutions. We will continue our work with multilateral institutions and through the Development Assistance Committee of the OECD to encourage a similar shift in the focus of development assistance globally.

288. Development assistance continues to have an important role in middle income countries, where there are large numbers of people still living in poverty. Many of these countries have considerable resources of their own and access to private sector investment. They do not therefore need the large-scale concessional resource flows required by low income countries[20], but support to focus their own resources on the reforms needed to reduce poverty and inequality. There is an important role for technical assistance to improve the effectiveness of government and the efficiency of markets in order to achieve this.

289. The UK has particular responsibilities for Britain's remaining Overseas Territories[21]. We are committed to support them in adapting successfully to the opportunities and challenges of globalisation. We are also keen to assist them play their part in improving global financial stability.

290. While development assistance can contribute to poverty reduction in

---

[19] *Excluding humanitarian aid*

[20] *Most middle income countries also receive non-concessional flows from developed countries and the international financial institutions to compensate for the partial nature of their access to foreign private finance, particularly for social sector investment.*

[21] *Further details are provided in the Government White Paper, 'Partnership for Prosperity: Britain and the Overseas Territories', March 1999*

countries pursuing sound policies, large numbers of poor people live in countries – both low income and middle income – where these characteristics are absent. Almost 160 million people live in countries in which the policy environment is assessed as too weak for World Bank engagement. A further 288 million live in countries in which the World Bank is active but which it assesses as having a very poor policy environment[xxxvi].

291. Conventional government-to-government aid tends to be ineffective in such circumstances and may even help to perpetuate policies that hinder economic development. However, selective use of aid may still have an important role – in relieving the distress of the poor in the short-term and in helping to encourage social and political change. This includes both humanitarian assistance for those in dire need, and support for independent media, NGOs and other parts of civil society.

292. In some circumstances it may also be possible to work with local or regional governments or even individual Ministries that are pursuing good policies. Selective

BOX 14

GLOBAL PUBLIC GOODS

'Public goods' are goods which benefit society as a whole. The concept of 'national public goods', such as the maintenance of law and order, is not new. But in an increasingly interconnected and interdependent world much more attention is now being paid to 'global public goods'. Examples range from the control of communicable diseases, to the provision of global financial stability, the protection of the environment and the prevention of conflict.

These are all issues in which the international community has a common interest. Some are particularly important to poor countries and people. Action to combat global warming is an example. Developed countries are a major source of this through emissions of carbon dioxide. But the consequences are most severe in developing countries - as shown by the floods in Bangladesh and Mozambique.

In some cases, the key requirement is a commitment to closer international co-operation. In others more finance is needed too. In those cases where there is a clear link to the central task of poverty reduction, development assistance can be an appropriate source. But finding the right financing mechanisms - and the appropriate institutional framework - requires a case by case approach.

In some cases a co-ordinated approach through a shared public facility may be the best answer, such as the Global Environment Facility (GEF). There are also other opportunities to build coalitions between the public sector, private industry and voluntary foundations, to make a concerted attack on a specific global problem - as for example through the Global AIDS Vaccine Initiative (GAVI).

use of aid is likely to be more effective in building the foundations for change if countries ensure that their policies in other areas, such as trade and arms sales, are consistent with this agenda.

293. The current legislative basis for most of the UK's development assistance programme is the 1980 Overseas Development and Co-operation Act. This Act is outdated, reflecting a number of now discredited approaches to development. The Government is committed to introducing a new International Development Bill to consolidate our poverty-focused approach.

294. We will also use the legislation to broaden the range of activities the Government can support to further our development objectives. These might include the promotion of development awareness by groups outside government, the ability to take share-holdings in companies, and the use of guarantees to enable financial institutions to support high-risk small-scale activities We will publish a draft bill early in 2001.

Debt relief for poverty reduction

295. In many of the world's poorest countries the heavy burden of servicing debt reduces the resources available for tackling poverty and offsets the benefits of development assistance.

296. The UK has been at the forefront of international efforts to deliver substantial debt reduction to the poorest countries. The Heavily Indebted Poor Countries Initiative (HIPC) was launched in 1996 to address the problem of unsustainable debt. 41 countries were identified as potentially eligible for this exceptional relief.

297. A powerful international campaign – involving church and other faith groups and NGOs – led the call for more generous debt relief focused on poverty reduction. And this helped lead to agreement on an enhanced HIPC in 1999, that would deliver faster, deeper and wider debt relief. The focus of the HIPC Initiative was widened at this time from assisting countries to improve their economic position to ensuring that the debt relief process benefited the poor.

298. Debt relief is now being linked to national Poverty Reduction Strategies, that HIPC governments are preparing in consultation with civil society. The G7 summit in Cologne in 1999 pledged to deliver $100 billion in debt relief, through HIPC and traditional debt relief measures, including the cancellation of aid debts. This would cancel two-thirds of the debt owed by HIPC countries that could qualify for relief.

299. Progress has been made. A year after the revised HIPC Initiative had been agreed, ten countries were through to their Decision Point, the milestone at which they begin to receive debt relief. This meant that in one year, almost twice as much debt relief was pledged than in nearly four years under the previous initiative. Even though this represented greater progress than under previous initiatives, we have pressed strongly for the process to be accelerated. It has now been agreed that greater flexibility will be shown in assessing countries' eligibility for debt relief, with the focus on those conditions that are essential for poverty reduction and growth. The aim is to get 20 countries through by the end of 2000.

300. We are keen that the remaining HIPCs should qualify for their debt relief as soon as possible. However, there are a number of countries that are some way from qualifying for their HIPC relief – and the overwhelming reason for this is the persistence of violent conflict in these countries. This underlines the need to end conflict in many of the world's poorest countries if development is to take place.

301. The UK contributes financially to HIPC in two ways. The first is by writing off its own debts. The UK has pledged to go beyond the requirements of HIPC, and write off 100 per cent of the debts owed by HIPC countries as they pass through the process. UK aid debts worth £1.2 billion have already been cancelled. The remaining debts are owed to ECGD and the CDC, which total approximately £2 billion.

302. The second is by pledges to assist the multilateral development banks and the IMF with the costs of providing their share of debt relief. The UK has pledged $385 million, of which $316 million is for the HIPC Trust Fund, the second largest pledge of any country. The Trust Fund currently has $2.6 billion in total pledges. More will be needed, but we anticipate that the political will behind the process is sufficient to generate the necessary funding when it is required.

303. It is obviously important that once a country has received its debt relief, it avoids running up huge debts again. To help avoid this, the UK is helping countries develop their debt management expertise through its funding of the HIPC Capacity Building Programme. But responsible lending by creditor governments is also important.

304. As discussed in Chapter 4 (paragraph 208), ECGD is now committed to ensuring that guarantees for poor countries are not used for unproductive purposes. And this is being taken forward in the OECD. The international community also needs to ensure that it has effective means to assist countries facing external shocks, such as natural disasters or a marked decline in terms of trade, which can worsen a country's debt position. The UK is currently providing additional budgetary support for a number of countries in Africa which are suffering from a deterioration in their terms of trade, largely as a result of the increase in oil prices.

305. Debt relief for the HIPC countries is important, but it is not enough. Many other forms of assistance by the international community are needed to eliminate poverty. Moreover, huge numbers of people live in countries which are not highly indebted, particularly in south Asia. It is vital that their needs are not neglected as a result of our efforts to help the HIPC countries.

Nationally owned poverty reduction strategies

306. The international community has stated strongly that the rationale for debt relief is to allow countries to tackle poverty more effectively. At the meetings of the World Bank and the IMF in 1999, it was agreed, at UK prompting, that the support provided by the World Bank and the IMF to developing countries should be focused around poverty reduction strategies. These would be drawn up by the developing country government in consultation with its civil society.

307. This new approach will be applied not only to the Heavily Indebted Poor Countries, but is intended also to become the basis for all concessional resource flows from the World Bank and the IMF and other development agencies. Implementation has

so far focused on low income countries in Africa. We believe that the principle of a country-led poverty reduction strategy should apply to middle income countries and to other developing country regions too. But we recognise that the approach will need to vary according to national circumstances. What should not vary is a clear focus for the World Bank and IMF on poverty reduction. If achieved this will be a major reform.

308. The process of developing poverty reduction strategies is putting developing countries in the lead, devising and driving forward their own development strategies. But international support is conditional on economic, social and environmental policies which will systematically reduce poverty. The UK will work with other development agencies to provide support to at least 12 partner countries by 2004 to develop and implement poverty reduction strategies. The UK's country strategy papers will follow this approach, and will be broadened to address the full range of policy reforms needed to enable countries to adapt successfully to the challenges of globalisation.

309. The Poverty Reduction Strategy process is a response to a number of lessons drawn from development experience over recent decades. First, development co-operation requires a supportive policy environment: progress is next to impossible if the economic and political fundamentals are wrong. Second, over-prescriptive aid conditionality has a poor track record in persuading governments to reform their policies.

310. Third, development agencies themselves can be part of the problem. If development agency efforts are not set within a coherent development plan, the result can be wasteful duplication, inconsistency and ineffectiveness. This process also reflects the principles underlying the Comprehensive Development Framework – the importance of a long-term strategy led by the developing country, consulting with civil society and development agencies, and with a strong focus on results.

311. The UK Government is committed to working with others to build the capacity of governments to lead the formulation, implementation and monitoring of the Poverty Reduction Strategy process, and to ensure full participation of civil society. We will encourage development NGOs to strengthen their links with civil society in developing countries – so that faith groups in particular are empowered to lobby for a strong poverty reduction focus in government policy. We will continue to encourage the World Bank and the IMF to make the necessary changes to their own structures and working methods in a way

that is consistent with their commitment to the Poverty Reduction Strategy process.

312. The first Poverty Reduction Strategy papers (PRSPs) have so far focused on short-term goals. Clear targets for better economic management and poverty reduction will need to be matched with more specific policies and programmes. Future poverty strategies should be framed within the global economic context with links to trade, finance, investment and the new technologies and take full account of environment sustainability. PRSPs must also become implementation mechanisms for countries' long-term development strategies.

313. These are still early days. This process is new and radical. There have inevitably been practical difficulties with putting it into practice. But the UK Government believes that it represents an enormous conceptual shift from the structural adjustment of the 1980s and early 1990s. With continued support, this process could help to strengthen the international development community's contribution to poverty reduction and sustainable development.

Improving the way development agencies deliver assistance

314. If assistance is to help developing countries reduce poverty in a global economy, there needs to be a real improvement in the way that assistance is delivered. That means reducing support for stand-alone projects, and increasing support for sector-wide reforms[xxxvii]. Where governments have a strong commitment to poverty reduction and good policies in place, it means moving towards providing financial support directly to recipient government budgets using their own systems.

315. It also means helping to strengthen developing country planning, financial and procurement systems to provide the assurances necessary to enable development agencies to provide such direct budgetary support. Development agencies should simplify and harmonise their own procedures to reduce the burden imposed on developing countries. This will assist in building government systems that prevent corruption. The UK Government is committed to working in this way.

316. We have worked hard to promote greater harmonisation among development agencies. For example, we have worked very closely with Germany, the Netherlands and Norway in co-ordinating our development efforts in Tanzania using the sector-wide approach, as a model for how we and other development agencies might work elsewhere. We have also agreed to work with Sweden, Denmark and Norway in Malawi. We are keen to adopt this approach in other countries, and to involve other development agencies. Different approaches are required in countries where aid is a much smaller proportion of national income and where there is strong government commitment to

BOX 15

SIMPLIFYING AND HARMONISING DELIVERY OF DEVELOPMENT ASSISTANCE

We are working with other development agencies to reduce the burden on developing countries of the differing accountability requirements of individual agencies.

In Malawi four development agencies – UK, Sweden, Denmark and Norway — have agreed on a common mechanism for disbursing aid and joint reporting arrangements. Development assistance from all four agencies will be provided in support of the government's budget with the government reporting quarterly on expenditures. The four development agencies have committed to using simplified and common administrative procedures for disbursement, co-ordinating their requests for information and undertaking joint meetings.

In India we are developing effective partnerships with the World Bank and Asian Development Bank at state level. We are working alongside the World Bank with the Governments of Andhra Pradesh and Orissa to improve economic performance and deliver a greater level of resources in support of pro-poor polices in these states. If good progress is made on policy reform, we will consider providing financial aid through the state budget alongside World Bank loans. In Madhya Pradesh we are working in a similar way with the Asian Development Bank.

domestic planning processes. We are responding to these conditions in India by working with multilateral banks at a state level (see box 15).

317. All development agencies, including non-governmental organisations, should reduce the proliferation of small programmes. For developing countries, the bureaucracy involved in dealing with a plethora of different agencies ties up valuable administrative capacity and fails to encourage reforms in government effectiveness.

318. There needs to be greater transparency in the operation of all development programmes. Developing country governments should be involved in deciding how funds are allocated and be kept informed on commitments, disbursements and missions. And reviews of programmes should be broadened beyond other development agencies to representatives of developing countries and civil society.

319. The UK Government will follow these principles in our own programmes and push for a greater role to be played by developing country representatives in the Development Assistance Committee's peer reviews[22]. We will also encourage independent evaluations of the effectiveness of development agencies.

Untying aid and promoting local procurement

320. The UK Government is totally committed to the multilateral untying of aid. Tied aid is one of the most damaging carry-overs from the past. It is damaging for three reasons. The first is value for money. It is estimated that tying aid to the purchase of goods and services from the donor country reduces the value of that aid by around 25 per cent[xxxviii].

321. Second, it is grossly inefficient. It leads to developing countries being supplied with incompatible pieces of equipment provided by different development agencies, each with separate requirements for spares and back-up. For example a country committed to reform the effectiveness of its health sector is required to divide up procurement to fit the differing requirements of perhaps half a dozen development agencies rather than procure the most cost-effective supplies available.

322. Third, it encourages a donor driven approach to development. It signals that development agencies' major concern is not development, but their national contracts. This practice is inconsistent with the new approach to development co-operation encapsulated in the Poverty Reduction Strategy process.

---

[22] The Development Assistance Committee (DAC) conducts periodic reviews to improve the individual and collective development co-operation efforts of DAC members. The policies and efforts of individual members are critically examined approximately once every three years. Six programmes are examined annually.

323. It is for all these reasons that the UK Government has worked hard to reach international agreement on aid untying. To show our commitment to this objective and encourage others to follow the UK lead, we have in the meantime decided to untie all UK development assistance from 1 April 2001[xxxix]. Building on our commitment to aid untying, we will vigorously pursue successful completion of the agreement being negotiated with the OECD to untie financial assistance to the least developed countries from 1 January 2002. We will work for early and complete EU-wide untying of member states' bilateral aid, and will press this strongly both with the Commission and with other member states.

324. We will also work to strengthen procurement capacities in developing countries. Sound local procurement can bring real development benefits, by strengthening the local private sector and other local institutions. In addition, local procurement very often brings better value for money: goods that are more appropriate to local needs, services available on the spot, and reduced shipping costs and airfares.

Driving forward reform of European Community assistance

325. Around 30 per cent of the UK's aid budget is spent annually through the European Community's (EC) development programmes. In 1998 the EC was the fifth largest provider of aid, the largest provider of humanitarian assistance, and the largest multilateral grant provider. Taken together, EC programmes and the programmes of member states account for two-thirds of global development assistance.

326. But Europe's development effort currently falls well short of its potential and its capacity to be a force for good in the world. If Europe is to make a greater contribution to poverty reduction and the equitable management of globalisation, far-reaching reforms are needed.

327. The present Commission has acknowledged many of the weaknesses in existing programmes and begun to implement an ambitious reform agenda. The successor to the Lomé Convention – the Cotonou Agreement, signed by the European Union and 77 African, Caribbean and Pacific countries in June this year – now has poverty reduction as a central objective, as does the EC's new development policy statement.

328. The UK Government has worked strongly to generate support for the reform efforts. We also believe that it is disgraceful that the proportion of EC development aid going to low income countries has fallen from 75 per cent in 1987 to 51 per cent in 1997. Whereas a decade ago poor countries in Africa and Asia were the major recipients, now middle income countries have pushed most low income countries out of the top of the recipient list. The Government will work to increase the proportion of EC development aid allocated to low income countries – with a target of 70 per cent by 2006. We will also work to improve the targeting of EC aid in low and middle income countries on poverty reduction.

329. We welcome the Commission's intention to focus its programmes on sectors where it has a comparative advantage and efforts to develop new ways of working with the development banks. We welcome the proposals for improved management and evaluation of EC programmes, a better skills mix amongst staff, more decentralisation of decisions to the country level and more emphasis on monitoring outputs. And we are committed to working for greater coherence between the Commission's development policies and its policies on trade, investment, agriculture, finance and foreign policy[23].

Reforming the World Bank and the Regional Development Banks

330. The Development Banks - the World Bank and the Regional Development Banks for Africa, Asia, Latin America, Eastern Europe and the Caribbean – also play a central role in international development. Through the scale of their lending, and their expertise, they have considerable influence on the policies and priorities of their borrowing member countries.

331. The UK Government, which is a shareholder in all the Banks, is working to ensure that there is a clear focus on poverty reduction in their lending programmes. It is important that lending in middle income countries, many of which have substantial resources of their own and have access to private sector lending, is more focused on the reforms needed to reduce poverty and inequality.

332. We believe that the World Bank and the Regional Banks usefully complement each other. While the World Bank has a global perspective, the RDBs have a particular knowledge of, and loyalty from, countries in their region. But it is important for each to develop a better understanding of its comparative advantages and not duplicate effort.

333. At the institutional level, the development of a common understanding of respective roles – such as that between the World Bank and the African Development Bank – is a useful way forward. At the country level, we want to

---

[23] For a more detailed outline of the UK's policy towards the EC to promote the International Development Targets, see the DFID Strategy Paper: Working in Partnership with the European Community, DFID 1998. www.dfid.gov.uk.

see the Banks working better together and with other development partners, through the Comprehensive Development Framework and Poverty Reduction Strategy processes[24].

A more effective development role for the United Nations

334. The UN has an important role to play in poverty elimination both through its programmes and its ability to help build international consensus on development issues. In recent years, since the Secretary General launched his reform package, considerable progress has been made. The Millennium Assembly was a milestone in terms of gaining international recognition of the International Development Targets. But the current UN system is not as effective as it should be.

335. Each individual UN agency needs to identify and concentrate on its areas of comparative advantage in delivering the International Development Targets. The UN can help to promote greater co-ordination and coherence in the international system, through improving its own collaboration around country-led programmes and harmonisation of its administrative systems with other development agencies. Beyond this, the proliferation of independent, issue-based institutions creates a strong case for looking at the effectiveness of the overall structure of the UN system for meeting the challenges of the new millennium.

336. The UN has already taken steps to co-ordinate its work more effectively, through the UN Development Assistance Framework (UNDAF). But it is important, too, that the UN should collaborate more with other development agencies, notably the World Bank and regional development banks. This needs to become over time a coherent strategy for the UN system as a whole at country level, supporting countries' own poverty reduction strategies.

337. The UN's 2001 Financing For Development conference provides an opportunity to generate greater international understanding of how we can make better use of development assistance, government revenues, debt relief and domestic and foreign investment. Improved effectiveness will also help to win stronger public support for increased aid budgets.

---

[24] *For a more detailed outline of the UK's policy towards the World Bank Group and Regional Development Banks to promote the International Development Targets, see the DFID Strategy Papers: Working in Partnership with the World Bank Group, DFID 2000; Working in Partnership with the African Development Bank, DFID 2000; and Working in Partnership with the Asian Development Bank, DFID 2000. www.dfid.gov.uk.*

THE UK GOVERNMENT WILL:

- Ensure that UK development assistance as a proportion of GNP rises to 0.33 per cent by 2003/04 and continue to make progress towards the 0.7 per cent UN target.

- Introduce a new International Development Bill to replace the outdated Overseas Development and Co-operation Act (1980), to consolidate our poverty focused approach to development, and to broaden the range of activities that the Government can support.

- Allocate more of our development assistance to low income countries and promote a more poverty-focused approach to middle income countries.

- Broaden our country strategy papers to take account of all the policy reforms needed to enable countries to meet the challenges of globalisation.

- Work with other donors to channel more of our support through developing country budgetary systems, where governments have a strong commitment to poverty reduction, and help strengthen their planning, financial and procurement systems to make this possible.

- Work to simplify and harmonise aid delivery amongst development agencies collectively, and increase the transparency of development programmes.

- Untie all UK development assistance with effect from 1 April 2001.

- Vigorously pursue successful completion of the agreement being negotiated within the OECD to untie all forms of financial assistance to the least developed countries from 1 January 2002, and work vigorously for EU wide untying.

- Work for improvements in the effectiveness of EC development assistance with a target of 70 per cent of EC aid going to low income countries by 2006.

- Press the Development Banks to design programmes which focus on reducing poverty in all borrowing countries, and to clarify their comparative advantages.

- Press for a more co-ordinated approach by the UN system as a whole and a more effective focus on poverty reduction and collaboration with all parts of the international development system.

CHAPTER 8

STRENGTHENING THE INTERNATIONAL SYSTEM

The UK Government will:

- **Work with others to build a stronger, more open and accountable international system, in which poor people and countries have a more effective voice.**

Reforming international institutions

338. We live at a time of both opportunity and threat. Globalisation is generating massive new wealth, which creates the opportunity to reduce global poverty. But if it is not managed well, it could also pose a threat to stability and security across the world. If we are to make globalisation work better for poor people, we need a more effective, open and accountable international system. We need global political institutions to better manage and counterbalance global markets, and to help promote global social justice.

339. The international institutions have undergone significant reform over recent years. There is a growing commitment in the UN system to carry out its mandate on conflict resolution, and on development, more effectively. But much remains to be done. Similarly, the international financial institutions are increasingly strengthening their contribution to poverty reduction, but have the capacity to be more effective.

340. All of these institutions have now agreed to focus their efforts around the international development targets. But it is important that this commitment goes wider than the more effective use of aid resources. We need a focus on poverty reduction and greater coherence between policies on aid, trade, debt, investment, the environment, and conflict. And we need better co-ordination between all of the international institutions.

341. In this chapter we focus on how to enhance the overall contribution of the key institutions to poverty reduction, and on how to give developing countries a more effective voice within them. We also look at a number of other international institutions – the G8, the OECD and the Commonwealth – and suggest how they could contribute to making globalisation work better for the world's poor.

342. To increase their impact, many of these institutions require management reforms, as well as reforms to structures and working methods. We welcome the steps being taken by the UN Secretary-General to reform management practices and increase collaboration between UN development agencies. These reform agendas need to be driven forward more urgently.

343. There is also a need for continous attention to issues of accountability and transparency in all institutions. Significant progress has been made in the IMF, in particular a commitment to establish an independent evaluation office to look at all aspects of the IMF's business. But more effort is needed to share analysis and build capacity for dialogue with developing countries.

344. Important steps have been taken in the Multilateral Development Banks, including on disclosure policies, independent evaluation, inspection mechanisms, and policy compliance. Other areas need further work, including the relationship between boards and management.

345. In all of these institutions, the UK Government favours open and competitive processes for the selection of top management. This could include a definition of the competencies for the post, selection and search committees and a clear process for taking the final decision, in which competence would be put above considerations of nationality.

A more effective voice for poor countries and people

346. Developing countries are entitled to a stronger and more effective voice in all of these international institutions. In many, such as the WTO, they constitute the overwhelming majority of the membership, and, with greater organisation, would be well placed to exert their influence. Some of the larger developing countries already play a very effective role in international institutions. But some of the smaller and least developed countries need further support to strengthen their representation and negotiating capacity.

347. Developing countries can also secure a more effective international voice through regional organisations, which can be particularly important as advocates for smaller countries. For example, the Caribbean Regional Negotiating Machinery, supported by the UK, has enabled some of the smaller Caribbean states to negotiate very effectively with its EU and North American partners. The UK Government will work to strengthen regional organisations and in particular help to enhance their capacity to promote the interests of smaller countries.

Enlisting the G8, the OECD and the Commonwealth

348. The UK Government has worked within the G8 to put development issues higher on the agenda, ranging from debt relief and aid untying, to fighting HIV/AIDS, promoting renewable energy and closing the digital divide. We believe that the G8 has a duty to take forward action on these issues. We particularly welcome the

G8 decision to review annually progress towards the International Development Targets. We will seek to ensure that developing countries are fully involved in discussions with the G8 and the OECD on all initiatives affecting their interests.

349. The OECD has an important role to play. Earlier parts of this paper have referred to its work on transnationals, bribery and export credit. Its Development Assistance Committee (DAC) is a key forum in promoting the international development targets, better co-ordination of donor policies and procedures, and improvements in aid effectiveness. More generally, the OECD should become an important forum for integrating a development perspective into the analysis of key international economic issues. Progress has been made through the collaboration of its trade committee and the DAC. This should now be extended through all Directorates of the OECD.

350. The Commonwealth is a unique grouping, embracing developed, developing and least developed countries across all regions of the globe, and including many of the world's smallest countries. It is a valuable forum for addressing issues such as tax, competition, money laundering and corruption, as well as broader political issues such as good government. We will work to sharpen the focus of the Commonwealth's activities on its areas of comparative advantage.

Measuring progress

351. Good statistics tell us whether policy interventions are working or not, and which ones work better than others. They are critical for evidence-based policy-making. But good data is also crucial in mobilising political will. If we cannot tell with any accuracy whether development efforts are proving effective, the public have no way of judging progress. But if we can measure success and show where development works, we are much better placed to increase public support and the political will for further action.

352. There is currently a critical shortfall in the international and national effort devoted to developing statistical capacity. In recent years we have worked to increase the commitment to progress, and there have been some important steps forward. In 1999, at the G8 summit, it was agreed that progress against the International Development Targets should be measured annually. The IMF, World Bank, UN and the OECD launched the *Better World for All* report at the UN special session in Geneva in June 2000. This set out progress so far towards the International Development Targets and the further effort that is required to reach them. The UK is also providing support to a new international partnership in statistics for the 21st century (PARIS21) — a consortium established to help build statistical capacity in developing countries.

Strengthening the international response to conflict

353. A strengthened international system has a crucial role to play in dealing with violent conflict. The UN Secretary General has put conflict prevention at the top of his agenda. In many parts of the UN system there are signs of a willingness to try new approaches, and to work more collaboratively. Reviews and evaluations – including the Secretary General's reports on the genocide in Rwanda and the events in Srebrenica – have demonstrated a readiness to acknowledge past failure.

354. The UK is committed to working for a stronger UN contribution to conflict prevention, resolution and peace-building. We agree with the recommendations in the Brahimi Report on UN Peacekeeping[xl]. This Report calls for an overhaul of the management of UN peacekeeping operations in New York and a more robust posture by UN peacekeeping forces in the field. And it calls for better analysis of conflict situations, and better training and skills for UN officials involved in this area. It also calls for stronger inter-agency arrange-   ments   for   planning, implementation and co-ordinating conflict-related activities and for improvements in the performance of in-country UN peace making and peace building missions, especially the efforts of the Special Representatives of the Secretary General.

The UK Government believes that the Brahimi Report should be implemented within 12 months[xli]. We also believe that there is an important role for regional organisations in conflict prevention, resolutions and peace-building.

355. Where there are large-scale violations of international humanitarian law and crimes against humanity, and where the government in question is unable or unwilling to halt the atrocities, the UK believes that the international community should take action. The action may take a number of forms. Once all non-violent measures have been exhausted, it may, in exceptional circumstances, be necessary and appropriate to use force to achieve the humanitarian purpose. Kosovo and East Timor are two recent examples.

356. We would wish to see the Security Council, acting on behalf of all UN members, take the lead in responding to such humanitarian catastrophes. The UK remains at the forefront of efforts to build international consensus on the conditions and circumstances when the Security Council should authorise intervention for humanitarian purposes.

357. When violent conflicts end, it is also vital that the international community should support the conditions for sustainable peace. Without such support, many post-conflict societies are liable to fall back into conflict. We will work with other development agencies and international institutions to support improved post-conflict reconstruction and peace building, including disarmament, demobilisation and reintegration programmes.

358. We will work with others in such countries to help rebuild inclusive political institutions. It is often the absence or weakness of these institutions – and therefore the absence of any means of resolving tensions and conflicts peacefully – that leads to violence.

359. We fully support the establishment of the International Criminal Court (ICC) and are bringing forward legislation to ratify the Rome Statute. The ICC will be a major advance for international humanitarian and human rights law. Once established, it will help to end impunity for gross human rights violations and for war crimes. Bringing to justice those responsible for serious crimes against humanity can help promote the prospect of reconciliation in countries that have been scarred by violent conflict.

Mobilising civil society

360. If the international system is to work for poor people, we need stronger national and global civil society demanding the changes necessary to deliver the International Development Targets. The spread of democracy across the world has created an opportunity for progress.

361. It is particularly important to strengthen the voices of civil society in developing countries. The Voices of the Poor consultation showed that poor people place their greatest trust in churches and faith groups. But other groups – human rights and women's organisations, trade unions, NGOs and co-operatives – could also play a stronger role in giving poor people a greater voice.

362. There is also an important role for civil society in developed countries. The UK Government works closely and constructively with NGOs and other elements of UK civil society. However, we are also committed to improving the transparency and accountability of NGOs and other parts of civil society, to the people on whose behalf they speak.

363. We will continue to give priority to development education and awareness, and will work to strengthen public understanding of globalisation and sustainable development. Early in the next Parliament we will hold a further round of Development Policy Forums across the UK, involving groups and individuals from

BOX 16

DEVELOPMENT POLICY FORUMS

Following the 1997 White Paper on International Development the UK Government organised two rounds of full-day discussions across the UK on development issues. Participants were drawn from NGOs, trade unions, ethnic minority groups, businesses, local government, community groups and the faiths, as well as Ministers and officials from a number of government departments. The discussions were intended as an opportunity to listen to a wide variety of views, to discuss government policy and to build support for development. Globalisation will be a key issue for future Forums.

across society (see box 16). We have worked to ensure that the revised national curriculum in England incorporates a commitment to sustainable development and a global dimension in education. We will now focus our efforts on providing appropriate guidance and support for teachers. We are undertaking similar work in Scotland, Wales and Northern Ireland.

364. We will continue to develop our public information and consultation work, so that young people in particular have a better understanding of the world they will inherit. We are also committed to publishing, as part of the annual Departmental Report of the Department for International Development, an account of progress towards the International Development Targets, which could form the basis for regular Parliamentary debates.

Making globalisation work for the poor

365. Making globalisation work for the world's poor is the greatest moral challenge facing our generation. The new millennium brings to humanity both the real prospect of meeting the International Development Targets by 2015, and the capacity to eliminate global poverty completely in the course of the century.

366. Our ambitions must match that potential. The institutions and governments of the international system must be held to account for their effectiveness – above all, their effectiveness in managing the forces of globalisation for the benefit of those who are born into deprivation, squalor and poverty.

367. The policies set out in this White Paper will ensure that the UK continues to work to this end. They will increase social justice. They are also in the UK's self-interest because they will contribute to a more stable and prosperous world at a time when no country can be isolated from global developments. The Government will take them forward with vigour and determination.

THE UK GOVERNMENT WILL:

- Support open and competitive processes for the selection of the top management of international institutions.

- Work to strengthen the development efforts of the G8, the OECD and the Commonwealth, and for G8 and OECD decisions to take greater account of developing country interests.

- Support the development of international and national statistical capacity, so that we can measure progress against the International Development Targets.

- Work to enhance and improve the effectiveness the UN's role in conflict prevention and peace-building, and to secure agreement to the implementation of the Brahimi Report within 12 months.

- Bring forward legislation to ratify the Rome Statute of the International Criminal Court and encourage other countries to do so.

- Work with civil society to strengthen the capacity of poor people to hold governments and international institutions to account for progress on poverty reduction.

- Build on our successful programme of Development Policy Forums with a further round focused on globalisation and poverty in the new Parliament.

- Publish an account of progress towards the International Development Targets, which could form the basis for regular parliamentary debates.

i   UN Secretary General, April 2000, *Report to the Millennium Assembly.*

ii   UNDP, 1999, *Human Development Report*; UN Secretary General, April 2000, *Report to the Millennium Assembly,* World Bank, June 2000, *World Development Report 2000/01.*

iii UN Secretary General, April 2000, *Report to the Millennium Assembly.*

iv   UNHCS, 1999, *An Urbanising World, Global Report on Human Settlements.*

v   The evidence in paragraphs 27-34 is drawn mainly from:
     a. UNCTAD 1996, *Report on Least Developed Countries;*
     b. Crafts, Nicholas, March 2000, *Globalisation and Growth in the Twentieth Century,* IMF Working Paper;
     c. Dollar, David and Kraay, Aart, March 2000, *Growth is Good for the Poor;*
     d. White, Howard and Anderson, Edward, 2000, *Growth Vs Distribution: Does the Pattern of Growth Matter?;*
     e. Ravallion, Martin, July 2000, *Growth and Poverty: Making Sense of the Current Debate;*
     f. Cornia, Giovanni Andrea, 2000, *Inequality and Poverty in the Era of Liberation and Globalisation,* UNU/WIDER.

vi   World Bank, 2000, *Voices of the Poor Study.* This was based on the experiences of more than 60,000 poor women and men in 60 countries, as background for the *World Development Report 2000/2001.*

vii Worldaware/Commonwealth Business Council Report *Priorities for Action to Promote Investment in the Commonwealth;* Smarzynska, B and Wei, Shiang Jin, March 2000, *Corruption and Composition of Foreign Direct Investment* US National Bureau of Economic Research Report.

viii Cabinet Office, 2000, *Report on Recovering the Proceeds of Crime.*

ix   *A Better World for All,* 2000.

x   Secretary of State for Trade and Industry, Stephen Byers.

xi   Sachs, Jeffrey and London School of Hygiene and Tropical Medicine, 2000.

xii The data in this box are drawn from: World Bank Policy Research Report: *Confronting AIDS. Public priorities in a global epidemic* and UNAIDS Report on the global HIV/AIDS epidemic, June 2000, *Waking up to devastation.*

xiii UNESCO, 2000, Statistical Document *Education for All Assessment.* World Education Forum.

xiv KPMG, 2000 *The Impact of the New Economy on Poor People.*

xv   OECD, 2000, *E-Commerce for Development: Prospects and Policy Issues.*

xvi This is based on analysis done by John Weeks at the School of Oriental and African Studies (unpublished).

xvii Global Forum for Health Research, 1999: *The 10/90 Report on Health Research.*

xviii This will be published in a Cabinet Office Report: *HIV/AIDS, Tuberculosis and Malaria in Developing Countries: Harnessing the Contribution of the Private Sector.*

xix The data in paragraphs 149-152 are drawn from IMF World Economic Outlook, September 2000.

xx   Collier, Paul, Hoeffler, Anke and Pattulo, Catherine, December 1999, *Flight Capital as a Portfolio Choice,* IMF Working Paper.

xxi Victor Welnikov, Deputy Governor of the Russian Central Bank.

xxii Oxfam, June 2000, *Tax Havens: Releasing the Hidden Billions for Poverty Eradication.*

xxiii Pensions and Investment Research Consultants Ltd. 2000, *Assessment of a Proposal to Encourage Triple Bottom Line Reporting.*

xxiv Inamdar, Amar, *Improving the Developmental Impact of Transnational Corporations,* Synergy.

xxv Cabinet Office Report, September 2000, *Rights of Exchange: Social, Health, Environmental and Trade Objectives on the Global Stage.*

xxvi McKay, Andrew, Winters, L Alan and Mamo Kedir, Abbi, June 2000, *A Review of Empirical Evidence on Trade, Trade Policy and Poverty.* CREDIT.

xxvii Mayer, Jorg and Wood, Adrian, forthcoming, *South Asia's export structure in a comparative perspective,* Oxford Development Studies.

xxviii Nichols, Lucy, 1991 "Human resources and structural adjustment: evidence from Costa Rica", in Martin Godfrey (ed), *Skill Development for International Competitiveness;* Rodriguez, Ennio, 1997, "Costa Rica: policies and conditions for export diversification", Inter-American Development Bank.

SOURCE NOTES

xxix Nagarajan, Nigel, November 1999, *The Millennium Round: An Economic Appraisal,* European Commission Economic Papers.

xxx European Commission, 1997, Green Paper on *Relations Between the European Union and the ACP countries on the Eve of 21st Century: Challenges and Options for a New Partnership.*

xxxi Milner, C., Morrissey, Oliver and Rudaheranwa, N, 2000 (forthcoming), "Policy and Non-Policy Barriers to Trade and Implicit Taxation of Exports in Uganda", *Journal of Development Studies.*

xxxii Limao, Nuno and Venables, Anthony, 1999, *Infrastructure, Geographical Disadvantage and Transport Costs,* Columbia University and LSE.

xxxiii Prime Minister's Speech to the CBI/Green Alliance Conference on the Environment, 24 October 2000, *Richer and Greener.*

xxxiv Collier, Paul and Dollar, David, March 2000, *Can the World Cut Poverty in Half?* and Dollar,David, May 2000, *Some Thoughts on the Effectiveness of Aid, Non-Aid Development Finance and Technical Assistance* (nb. the 50% increase is based on constraining the allocation to India - if this is relaxed the figure increases to 90%).

xxxv Dollar, David & Burnside, Craig, 1988, *Assessing Aid - What Works and What Doesn't and Why,* World Bank.

xxxvi World Bank's Country Policy and Institutional Assessment table 1998.

xxxvii Foster, Mick, June 2000, *Experience with Implementing Sector Wide Approaches,* ODI

xxxviii Dollar, David & Burnside, Craig, 1988, *Assessing Aid - What Works and What Doesn't and Why,* World Bank.

xxxix UK Statistics on Untying 2000. Most UK aid is already untied. The tied proportion of UK commitments of bilateral official development assistance (excluding Technical Cooperation) fell from 28% in 1997 to 8½% in 1999. The largest element of Technical Cooperation is consultancies (around £200 million). Other elements include: volunteers and other personnel; training and scholarships; knowledge and research. An increasing proportion of this is being procured in recipient countries.

xl Brahimi, August 2000, *Report of the Panel on United Nations Peacekeeping.*

xli Prime Minister, Tony Blair, September 2000: Speech to the Millennium Summit of the United Nations.

A Glossary and Bibliography can be found on www.globalisation.gov.uk

The following papers were commissioned by DFID as background research for the White Paper in 2000.

The content and views expressed in these papers do not necessarily reflect the views of the UK Government.

These papers are all available on the White Paper website: www.globalisation.gov.uk

Bennell, Paul, *Human Resources Development and Globalisation: What Should Low Income Developing Countries Do?*

Cobham, Alex, *The New International Financial Architecture, 'Codes and Standards' and the Developing Countries,* Queen Elizabeth House.

Conlin, Sean, and Norton, Andy, *Globalisation Processes and the Implications for the Development of Global Responses in the Field of Social Policy,* CAPE, Overseas Development Institute.

Dollar, David, *Some Thoughts on the Effectiveness of Aid, Non-Aid Development Finance and Technical Assistance,* World Bank.

Development Initiatives, *Global Development Assistance: The Role of Non-Governmental Organisations and Other Charity Flows.*

DFID, *Globalisation, Governance and Poverty Reduction.*

DFID, *Governments and E-information and Communication Technologies in Development.*

DFID, *Global Health and Development: The Impact of Globalisation on the Health of Poor People.*

DFID, *An Overview: Financial Flows and Developing Countries.*

Fitzgerald, Valpy, and Cobham, Alex, *Capital Flight: Causes, Effects, Magnitude and Implications,* Queen Elizabeth House.

Fitzgerald, Valpy, and Cobham, Alex, *Meitzer: Is There Still a Case for Public Banks?,* Queen Elizabeth House.

Fitzgerald, Valpy, and Cobham, Alex, *A Waste of Development?: the Volatility and Pro-Cyclicality of Official Flows to Developing Countries,* Queen Elizabeth House.

Foster, Mick, and Chalinder, Paula, *Strategies for Sustainable Development: Will Country Led Frameworks Sustain Poverty Elimination?* Overseas Development Institute.

Foster, Mick, *Experience with Implementing Sector Wide Approaches* CAPE, Overseas Development Institute.

Hyvarinen, Joy, and Brack, Duncan, *Global Environmental Institutions: Analysis and Options for Change,* Royal Institute for International Affairs.

Inamdar, Amar, *Improving the Developmental Impact of Transnational Corporations,* Synergy.

KPMG, *The Impact of the New Economy on Poor People and Developing Countries.*

Mavrotas, George, *The Impact of Aid on Private Savings and Investment,* Oxford Policy Management.

McKay, Andrew, Winters, L Alan, and Mamo Kadir, Abbi, *A Review of Empirical Evidence on Trade, Trade Policy and Poverty,* CREDIT.

Morrissey, Oliver, *Case Studies of the Poverty Experience in Economies Undergoing Economic Adjustment,* CREDIT and Overseas Development Institute.

Muggeridge, Liz, Sheehey, Tim, and Godfrey, Steve, *Promoting Effective Participation in PRSPs.*

Norton, Andy, Conway, Tim and Foster, Mick, *Social Protection Concepts and Approaches,* CAPE, Overseas Development Institute.

Page, Sheila, *Trends in Developing Country Trade 1980-1999,* Overseas Development Institute.

Page, Sheila, *Developing Countries' Integration into the World Economy.* Overseas Development Institute.

Page, Sheila, *Prospects for Developing Country Trade.* Overseas Development Institute.

Perraton, Hilary, *Information and Communications Technologies for Education in the South.*

Royal Institute for Internation Affairs, *Global Environmental Governance.*

Skuse, Andrew, *Information Communication Technologies, Poverty and Empowerment,* DFID.

Stevens, Christopher, and Kennan, Jane, *Analysis of EU Trade Arrangements with Developing and Transition Economies,* Institute of Development Studies.

White, Howard, and Anderson, Edward, *Growth vs. Distribution: Does the Pattern of Growth Matter?,* Institute of Development Studies.

Printed in the UK for The Stationary Office Limited
On behalf of the Controller of Her Majesty's Stationary Office
Dd5069512, 12/00, 5673, TJ003168